FAVORITE BRAND

I could go for so... ...ing

JELL-O®

BRAND

I could go for something

JELL-O®

BRAND

I Could Go For Something JELL-O

For more than 100 years, Jell-O has adapted to changes in lifestyles and eating habits—becoming a brand recognized by 99 percent of Americans and used regularly in nearly every home in America. With more than 125 varieties of snacks and desserts that can help make every day just a little sweeter, it's no wonder that Jell-O is "America's Most Famous Dessert™." This year continues the tradition of creating innovative, fun desserts and snacks with another spectacular collection of Jell-O recipes that are sure to please.

The possibilities are endless with gelatin. It can be served plain, combined with fruit and whipped topping in a parfait or concentrated into a fun Jiggler snack. Sparkling Jell-O can be mixed with club soda or tantalize the tongue and create shimmering molds.

The JELL-O team has been busy this year creating new recipes like Juicy Jell-O. Instead of **cold water,** you can now juice up your gelatin with fruit juices like white grape, apple or orange to create a more intense flavor. Juicy gelatin can be prepared in molds, special dessert cups or glasses or served cubed in parfaits. It's a great new way to personalize your favorite gelatin treat!

Pudding offers creamy indulgence for every day. With just two cups of milk, any flavor of instant Jell-O pudding and a quick stir, you can make a homemade snack in only five minutes. Plus, you can mix in marshmallows, cookies, candy or nuts for instant variety. Cooked pudding offers even more indulgence and can be prepared in minutes in popular flavors including Tapioca and Rice Pudding. Pudding is also a wonderful filling for cakes and pies, and a necessity when making pudding snack cups or frozen desserts.

Need to impress friends and family with a wow dessert? Jell-O No Bake Desserts take just 15 minutes with no baking. And in a variety of flavors, these easy-to-make desserts are a great way to dazzle your guests.

Delicious desserts and snacks used to take hours to make, but Jell-O brings you hundreds of ideas and products to make each day just a little sweeter, without spending hours in the kitchen.

On the following pages you'll find a delicious variety of recipes that are sure to answer the call for something sweet. For more information, we invite you to browse through the Jell-O Web site at www.jello.com to find even more ideas. When you can go for something sweet, creamy, fun or festive...remember to go for something Jell-O.

Prepare Jell-O Gelatin as directed in Basic Directions on Jell-O Gelatin Package, replacing <u>cold</u> water with cold fruit juice.

"Juicy JELL-O"	JELL-O Gelatin Flavor	Juice Flavor
Outrageous Orange	orange, lemon *or* lime	orange guava juice
Berry-Bop	strawberry	pineapple orange strawberry
Tutti-Frutti	strawberry banana, cherry *or* mixed fruit	pineapple *or* pinapple orange banana
Peach Passion	peach, apricot *or* lemon	orange peach mango
Berry Sensation	wild strawberry, raspberry *or* mixed fruit	raspberry kiwi
Sunshine Fun	strawberry kiwi, cranberry raspberry *or* orange	orange
Island Paradise	raspberry *or* peach	tropical fruit
Double Orange Berry	orange	orange strawberry banana
Hawaiian Luau	pineapple, orange *or* lemon	pineapple orange *or* pineapple orange banana
Krazy Kid Kups	berry blue, cherry *or* watermelon	orange strawberry banana

Shimmering Molds

Mimosa Mold

1½ cups boiling water
1 package (8-serving size) or 2 packages (4-serving size) JELL-O®
    Brand Sparkling White Grape or Lemon Flavor Gelatin Dessert
2 cups cold seltzer or club soda
1 can (11 ounces) mandarin orange segments, drained
1 cup sliced strawberries

STIR boiling water into gelatin in large bowl at least 2 minutes or until completely dissolved. Refrigerate 15 minutes. Gently stir in seltzer. Refrigerate about 30 minutes or until slightly thickened (consistency of unbeaten egg whites.) Gently stir about 15 seconds. Stir in oranges and strawberries. Pour into 6-cup mold.

REFRIGERATE 4 hours or until firm. Unmold. Garnish as desired. Store leftover gelatin mold in refrigerator.   *Makes 12 servings*

Preparation Time: 15 minutes
Refrigerating Time: 4¾ hours

Mimosa Mold

Melon Salad

A wonderful summer refresher.

2½ cups boiling apple juice
1 package (8-serving size) or 2 packages (4-serving size) JELL-O®
   Brand Watermelon Flavor Sugar Free Low Calorie Gelatin
   Dessert or JELL-O® Brand Watermelon Flavor Gelatin Dessert
1½ cups cold seltzer or club soda
1 teaspoon lemon juice
2 cups cantaloupe and honeydew melon cubes

STIR boiling juice into gelatin in large bowl at least 2 minutes until completely dissolved. Stir in cold seltzer and lemon juice. Refrigerate about 1½ hours or until thickened (spoon drawn through leaves definite impression). Stir in melon cubes. Spoon into 6-cup mold.

REFRIGERATE 4 hours or until firm. Unmold. Garnish as desired.

Makes 10 servings

Preparation Time: 15 minutes
Refrigerating Time: 5½ hours

JELL-O® Fun Facts

This flavorful watermelon gelatin was introduced in 1990 to appeal to kids but has become a hit with adults as well. It's especially refreshing with fresh summer fruits. Any red flavor gelatin may be substituted for the watermelon, if desired.

Melon Salad

Sunset Yogurt Mold

2 cups boiling water
1 package (8-serving size) or 2 packages (4-serving size) JELL-O®
    Brand Orange Flavor Sugar Free Low Calorie Gelatin Dessert
    or JELL-O® Brand Orange Flavor Gelatin Dessert
¼ cup cold water
1 can (8 ounces) crushed pineapple in juice, undrained
1 cup grated carrots
1 container (8 ounces) BREYERS® Vanilla Lowfat Yogurt

STIR boiling water into gelatin in large bowl at least 2 minutes until
completely dissolved. Reserve 1 cup gelatin at room temperature. Stir
cold water, pineapple with juice and carrots into remaining gelatin.
Spoon into 5-cup mold. Refrigerate about 2 hours or until set but not
firm (gelatin should stick to finger when touched and should mound).

STIR yogurt into reserved 1 cup gelatin with wire whisk until smooth.
Pour over gelatin layer in mold.

REFRIGERATE 4 hours or until firm. Unmold.   *Makes 10 servings*

Preparation Time: 20 minutes
Refrigerating Time: 6 hours

JELL-O® *Fun Facts*

*This pineapple carrot salad, developed in
1977, is one that guests will always
appreciate. JELL-O gelatin molds are great
served as either a side dish or dessert. This
mold can be served either way.*

Mandarin Orange Mold

2 cups boiling water
1 package (8-serving size) or 2 packages (4-serving size) JELL-O®
    Brand Orange Flavor Sugar Free Low Calorie Gelatin Dessert
    or JELL-O® Brand Orange Flavor Gelatin Dessert
¾ cup cold water
1 can (11 ounces) mandarin orange segments in juice, drained
1 container (8 ounces) BREYERS® Vanilla Lowfat Yogurt

STIR boiling water into gelatin in large bowl at least 2 minutes until completely dissolved. Reserve 1 cup gelatin at room temperature. Stir cold water and oranges into remaining gelatin. Pour into 5-cup mold. Refrigerate about 2 hours until set but not firm (gelatin should stick to finger when touched and should mound).

STIR yogurt into reserved 1 cup gelatin with wire whisk until smooth. Pour over gelatin layer in mold.

REFRIGERATE 4 hours or until firm. Unmold.   *Makes 10 servings*

Preparation Time: 20 minutes
Refrigerating Time: 6 hours

Sparkling Berry Salad

This berry-filled mold captures the freshness of spring.

> 2 cups boiling diet cranberry juice cocktail
> 1 package (8-serving size) or 2 packages (4-serving size) JELL-O®
>   Brand Sugar Free Low Calorie Gelatin Dessert or JELL-O®
>   Brand Gelatin Dessert, any red flavor
> 1½ cups cold seltzer or club soda
> ¼ cup creme de cassis liqueur (optional)
> 1 teaspoon lemon juice
> 3 cups assorted berries (blueberries, raspberries and sliced
>   strawberries), divided

STIR boiling cranberry juice into gelatin in large bowl at least 2 minutes until completely dissolved. Stir in cold seltzer, liqueur and lemon juice. Refrigerate about 1½ hours or until slightly thickened (consistency of unbeaten egg whites).

STIR in 2 cups of the berries. Spoon into 5-cup mold.

REFRIGERATE 4 hours or until firm. Unmold. Top with remaining 1 cup berries. *Makes 8 servings*

Preparation Time: 15 minutes
Refrigerating Time: 5½ hours

Fruit should be added to gelatin that has been chilled until it thickens, but is not yet set. This way the fruit will remain suspended in the gelatin.

Sparkling Berry Salad

Layered Orange Pineapple Mold

This creamy mold with a jewel-like crown goes beautifully with baked ham.

> 1 can (20 ounces) crushed pineapple in juice, undrained
> Cold water
> 1½ cups boiling water
> 1 package (8-serving size) or 2 packages (4-serving size) JELL-O®
>   Brand Orange Flavor Gelatin Dessert
> 1 package (8 ounces) PHILADELPHIA® Cream Cheese, softened

DRAIN pineapple, reserving juice. Add cold water to juice to make 1½ cups.

STIR boiling water into gelatin in large bowl at least 2 minutes until completely dissolved. Stir in measured pineapple juice and water. Reserve 1 cup gelatin at room temperature.

STIR ½ of the crushed pineapple into remaining gelatin. Pour into 6-cup mold. Refrigerate about 2 hours or until set but not firm (gelatin should stick to finger when touched and should mound).

STIR reserved 1 cup gelatin gradually into cream cheese in medium bowl with wire whisk until smooth. Stir in remaining crushed pineapple. Pour over gelatin layer in mold.

REFRIGERATE 4 hours or until firm. Unmold. Garnish as desired.

Makes 10 servings

Preparation Time: 20 minutes
Refrigerating Time: 6 hours

Layered Orange Pineapple Mold

Snack Attacks

Juicy JELL-O®

1 cup boiling water
1 package (4-serving size) JELL-O® Brand Gelatin, any flavor
1 cup cold juice, any flavor

STIR boiling water into gelatin in medium bowl at least 2 minutes until completely dissolved. Stir in cold juice.

REFRIGERATE 4 hours or until firm.   *Makes 4 (½-cup) servings*

Note: Do not use fresh or frozen pineapple, kiwi, papaya or guava juice. Gelatin will not set.

Variation: For fruited Juicy JELL-O®, prepare as directed but refrigerate for just 30 minutes until slightly thickened. Stir in 1 cup raspberries, blueberries or chopped strawberries. Refrigerate 4 hours or until firm.

Preparation Time: 5 minutes plus refrigerating

Juicy JELL-O®

5-Minute Chocolate Banana Parfait

2 cups cold fat free milk
1 package (4-serving size) JELL-O® Chocolate Flavor Fat Free
    Sugar Free Instant Reduced Calorie Pudding
2 medium bananas, sliced
½ cup thawed COOL WHIP LITE® Whipped Topping
1 tablespoon chopped walnuts, optional

POUR milk into medium bowl. Add pudding mix. Beat with wire whisk 2 minutes.

SPOON ½ of pudding evenly into 4 dessert glasses. Layer with banana slices, whipped topping and remaining pudding.

GARNISH each serving with additional banana slices, whipped topping and walnuts, if desired. *Makes 4 servings*

Preparation Time: 5 minutes

Aquarium Cups

¾ cup boiling water
1 package (4-serving size) JELL-O® Brand Berry Blue Flavor
    Gelatin Dessert
½ cup cold water
    Ice cubes
    Gummy fish

STIR boiling water into gelatin in medium bowl at least 2 minutes until completely dissolved. Mix cold water and ice cubes to make 1¼ cups. Add to gelatin, stirring until slightly thickened. Remove any remaining ice. (If mixture is still thin, refrigerate until slightly thickened.)

POUR thickened gelatin into 4 dessert dishes. Suspend gummy fish in gelatin. Refrigerate 1 hour or until firm. *Makes 4 servings*

Preparation Time: 10 minutes
Refrigerating Time: 1 hour

5-Minute Chocolate Banana Parfaits

Pudding Café

The addition of flavored coffees to this creamy snack makes it a favorite with adults.

> **2 cups cold milk**
> **1 package (4-serving size) JELL-O® Chocolate or Vanilla Flavor Instant Pudding & Pie Filling**
> **¼ cup GENERAL FOODS INTERNATIONAL COFFEES®, any flavor**

POUR milk into medium bowl. Add pudding mix and flavored instant coffee. Beat with wire whisk 2 minutes. Refrigerate 2 hours or until ready to serve.

Makes 4 servings

Preparation Time: 5 minutes
Refrigerating Time: 2 hours

Cinnamon Chocolate Pudding

> **2 cups cold milk**
> **1 package (4-serving size) JELL-O® Chocolate Flavor Instant Pudding & Pie Filling**
> **½ teaspoon ground cinnamon**
> **½ cup thawed COOL WHIP® Whipped Topping**

POUR milk into medium bowl. Add pudding mix and cinnamon. Beat with wire whisk 1 minute. Gently stir in whipped topping. Spoon into dessert dishes.

REFRIGERATE until ready to serve.

Makes 5 servings

Preparation Time: 5 minutes
Refrigerating Time: 2 hours

Juicy Parfaits

2 cups boiling water, divided
1 package (4-serving size) JELL-O® Brand Raspberry Flavor Gelatin
   Dessert or any red flavor
1 package (4-serving size) JELL-O® Brand Lemon Flavor Gelatin
   Dessert or any non-red flavor
2 cups cold juice, any flavor, divided
1 tub (8 ounces) COOL WHIP® Whipped Topping, thawed

STIR 1 cup of the boiling water into each flavor gelatin in separate bowls at least 2 minutes until completely dissolved. Stir 1 cup cold juice into each bowl. Pour into separate 9×9-inch pans.

REFRIGERATE 4 hours or until firm. Cut each pan into ½-inch cubes. Layer alternating flavors and whipped topping into 8 dessert glasses. Garnish with additional whipped topping, if desired.

Makes 8 servings

Note: *Do not use fresh or frozen pineapple, kiwi, papaya or guava juice. Gelatin will not set.*

Preparation Time: 10 minutes
Refrigerating Time: 4 hours

Juice Up Your JELL-O

Fruity Gelatin Pops

These super after-school treats couldn't be easier!

> 1 cup boiling water
> 1 package (4-serving size) JELL-O® Brand Gelatin Dessert, any flavor
> ⅓ cup sugar
> 1⅓ cups cold juice, any flavor
> 6 (5-ounce) paper cups

STIR boiling water into gelatin and sugar in medium bowl at least 2 minutes until completely dissolved. Stir in cold juice. Pour into cups. Freeze about 2 hours or until almost firm. Insert wooden pop stick into each for handle.

FREEZE 5 hours or overnight until firm. To remove pop from cup, place bottom of cup under warm running water for 15 seconds. Press firmly on bottom of cup to release pop. (Do not twist or pull pop stick.) Store leftover pops in freezer up to 2 weeks.   *Makes 6 pops*

Outrageous Orange Pops: *Use 1 cup boiling water, JELL-O® Brand Orange Flavor Gelatin Dessert, ⅓ cup sugar and 1⅓ cups orange juice.*

Fruity Strawberry Pops: *Use 1 cup boiling water, JELL-O® Brand Strawberry Flavor Gelatin Dessert, ⅓ cup sugar, ⅔ cup cold water and ⅔ cup puréed strawberries.*

Fizzy Grape Pops: *Use 1 cup boiling water, JELL-O® Brand Sparkling White Grape Flavor Gelatin Dessert, 2 tablespoons sugar and 1½ cups carbonated grape beverage.*

Lemonade Pops: *Use 1 cup boiling water, JELL-O® Brand Lemon Flavor Gelatin Dessert, ⅓ cup sugar, 1 cup cold water and 2 tablespoons lemon juice.*

Iced Tea Pops: *Use 1 cup boiling water, JELL-O® Brand Lemon Flavor Gelatin Dessert, 2 tablespoons sugar and 1½ cups pre-sweetened iced tea.*

Preparation Time: 10 minutes
Freezing Time: 7 hours

Juice Up Your JELL-O

Fruity Gelatin Pops

Easy Pudding Milk Shake

In just minutes, you can whip up this creamy milk shake—enough for the entire family.

3 cups cold milk
1 package (4-serving size) JELL-O® Instant Pudding & Pie Filling, any flavor
1½ cups ice cream, any flavor

POUR milk into blender container. Add pudding mix and ice cream; cover. Blend on high speed 30 seconds or until smooth. Pour into glasses and garnish as desired. Serve immediately.   *Makes 5 servings*

Preparation Time: 5 minutes

Jell-O Jigglers® Snack Pops

Jigglers® on sticks—like lollipops!

1¼ cups boiling water
1 package (8-serving size) or 2 packages (4-serving size) JELL-O® Brand Gelatin Dessert, any flavor
4 (5-ounce) paper cups
6 plastic straws, cut in half

STIR boiling water into gelatin in medium bowl at least 3 minutes until completely dissolved. Cool 15 minutes at room temperature. Pour into cups.

REFRIGERATE 3 hours or until firm. Carefully peel away cups. Using a knife dipped in warm water, cut each gelatin cup horizontally into 3 round slices. Insert straw into each gelatin slice to resemble a lollipop.
Makes 12 pops

Preparation Time: 10 minutes
Refrigerating Time: 3 hours

Easy Pudding Milk Shakes

Juicy Berry Sorbet

¾ cup boiling water
1 package (4-serving size) JELL-O® Brand Raspberry or Strawberry
   Flavor Gelatin
½ cup sugar
2 cups cold juice, any flavor

STIR boiling water into gelatin and sugar in large bowl at least 2 minutes until completely dissolved. Stir in cold juice. Pour into 9-inch square pan.

FREEZE about 1 hour or until ice crystals form 1 inch around edges. Spoon into blender container; cover. Blend on high speed about 30 seconds or until smooth. Return to pan. Freeze 6 hours or overnight until firm. Scoop into dessert dishes. Store leftover sorbet in freezer.

Preparation Time: 10 minutes
Freezing Time: 7 hours

Strawberry Banana Smoothie

Satisfy the between-meal "hungries" with this yummy drink.

2 cups crushed ice
1 cup cold milk
1 package (4-serving size) JELL-O® Brand Strawberry Flavor
   Gelatin Dessert
1 container (8 ounces) BREYERS® Vanilla Lowfat Yogurt
1 large banana, cut into chunks

PLACE all ingredients in blender container; cover. Blend on high speed 30 seconds or until smooth. Serve immediately.   *Makes 4 servings*

Preparation Time: 5 minutes

Juicy Berry Sorbet

Frozen Pudding Cookiewiches®

Keep these treats on hand in the freezer for last-minute snacks.

 1½ cups cold milk
 ½ cup peanut butter
 1 package (4-serving size) JELL-O® Instant Pudding & Pie Filling,
  any flavor
 24 graham crackers
  Colored sprinkles

STIR milk gradually into peanut butter in deep narrow bottomed bowl until smooth. Add pudding mix. Beat with wire whisk 2 minutes. Let stand 5 minutes.

SPREAD pudding mixture about ½-inch thick onto 12 of the crackers. Top with remaining crackers, pressing lightly and smoothing around edges with spatula. Coat edges with sprinkles.

FREEZE 3 hours or until firm.   *Makes 12*

Preparation Time: 15 minutes
Freezing Time: 3 hours

Pudding Mix-Ins

 2 cups cold milk
 1 package (4-serving size) JELL-O® Instant Pudding & Pie Filling,
  any flavor
  Assorted "treasures": BAKER'S® Semi-Sweet Real Chocolate
  Chips, chopped nuts, miniature marshmallows, raisins,
  chopped bananas, halved grapes, crumbled chocolate sandwich
  cookies or peanut butter
  Thawed COOL WHIP® Whipped Topping

POUR milk into medium bowl. Add pudding mix. Beat with wire whisk 2 minutes.

PLACE 1 tablespoon of the "treasures" into each of 4 dessert glasses. Spoon pudding over treasures.

REFRIGERATE until ready to serve. Top with whipped topping and garnish as desired.   *Makes 4 servings*

Preparation Time: 5 minutes
Refrigerating Time: 2 hours

Florida Sunshine Cups

¾ cup boiling water
1 package (4-serving size) JELL-O® Brand Sugar Free Low Calorie Orange or Lemon Flavor Gelatin
1 cup cold orange juice, any variety
½ cup fresh raspberries
½ cup fresh orange sections, halved

STIR boiling water into gelatin in large bowl at least 2 minutes until completely dissolved. Stir in cold juice. Refrigerate 1½ hours or until thickened (spoon drawn through leaves definite impression).

MEASURE ¾ cup thickened gelatin into medium bowl; set aside. Stir fruit into remaining gelatin. Pour into serving bowl or 6 dessert dishes.

BEAT reserved gelatin with electric mixer on high speed until fluffy and about doubled in volume. Spoon over gelatin in bowl or dishes.

REFRIGERATE 3 hours or until firm. Store leftover gelatin in refrigerator.   *Makes 6 servings*

Preparation Time: 20 minutes
Refrigerating Time: 4½ hours

5-Minute Mousse

1½ cups cold milk
1 package (4-serving size) JELL-O® Instant Pudding & Pie Filling, any flavor
1½ cups thawed COOL WHIP® Whipped Topping, divided

POUR milk into large bowl. Add pudding mix. Beat with wire whisk 2 minutes.

STIR in 1 cup whipped topping. Spoon into individual dessert dishes or serving bowl.

REFRIGERATE until ready to serve. Top with remaining whipped topping and garnish as desired. *Makes 5 servings*

Variation: Prepare recipe as directed above using fat free milk, any flavor JELL-O® Fat Free Sugar Free Instant Reduced Calorie Pudding & Pie Filling and COOL WHIP FREE® or COOL WHIP LITE® Whipped Topping.

Preparation Time: 5 minutes
Refrigerating Time: 2 hours

JELL-O® Fun Facts

For an extra decadent treat, drizzle this no-fuss mousse with your favorite chocolate fudge or caramel sauce and garnish with a rich store-bought chocolate-covered cookie. Your guests will be impressed!

5-Minute Mousse

Chocolate Peanut Butter Parfaits

Yummm! Luscious layers of two favorite flavors.

   3 tablespoons milk
   3 tablespoons peanut butter
   1 cup thawed COOL WHIP® Whipped Topping
   2 cups cold milk
   1 package (4-serving size) JELL-O® Chocolate Flavor Instant
        Pudding & Pie Filling
   ¼ cup chopped peanuts

STIR 3 tablespoons milk into peanut butter in medium bowl until smooth. Gently stir in whipped topping.

POUR 2 cups milk into medium bowl. Add pudding mix. Beat with wire whisk 2 minutes. Alternately spoon whipped topping mixture and pudding into 6 parfait glasses.

REFRIGERATE until ready to serve. Sprinkle with peanuts.

Makes 6 servings

Preparation Time: 5 minutes

JELL-O Fun Facts

For a fast, fabulous and refreshing version of this recipe, substitute JELL-O Lemon Flavor Instant Pudding for the chocolate pudding and prepare as above, omitting the peanut butter and 3 tablespoons milk from the Cool Whip mixture. Sprinkle with your favorite fresh fruit instead of peanuts!

Chocolate Peanut Butter Parfaits

Frozen Creamy Pudding Pops

1½ cups cold milk

1 package (4-serving size) JELL-O® Instant Pudding & Pie Filling, any flavor

2 cups thawed COOL WHIP® Whipped Topping

9 (5-ounce) paper or plastic cups or popsicle molds

ADDITIONS

½ cup chopped cookies

½ cup chopped toffee candy

½ cup mashed banana

½ cup miniature marshmallows and ¼ cup each chopped peanuts and BAKER'S Semi-Sweet Real Chocolate Chips

POUR milk into medium bowl. Add pudding mix. Beat with wire whisk 2 minutes. Gently stir in whipped topping. Stir in desired Special Additions. Spoon into cups. Insert wooden pop stick into each for handle.

FREEZE 5 hours or overnight. To remove pop from cup, place bottom of cup under running water for 15 seconds. Press firmly on bottom of cup to release pop. (Do not twist or pull pop stick.) *Makes 9 pops*

Special Additions: *Stir in ¼ cup GENERAL FOODS INTERNATIONAL COFFEES®, any flavor, with pudding mix.*

Preparation Time: 10 minutes

For a quick twist on this recipe, make pops in ice cube trays in different flavors and place in a large glass bowl for a fun "kids" table centerpiece. For a variation, add fresh blueberries or chopped strawberries to pops or cubes.

Buried Treasures

2 cups cold milk
1 package (4-serving size) JELL-O Instant Pudding & Pie Filling, any flavor
Assorted "treasures": BAKER'S Semi-Sweet Real Chocolate Chips, chopped nuts, miniature marshmallows, raisins, chopped bananas, halved grapes, crumbled chocolate sandwich cookies or peanut butter
Thawed COOL WHIP Whipped Topping

POUR milk into medium bowl. Add pudding mix. Beat with wire whisk 2 minutes.

PLACE 1 tablespoon of the "treasures" into each of 4 dessert glasses. Spoon pudding over treasures.

REFRIGERATE until ready to serve. Top with whipped topping and garnish as desired. *Makes 4 servings*

Preparation Time: 15 minutes
Refrigerating Time: 2 hours

JELL-O® Juicy Jigglers®

2½ cups boiling juice (Do not add cold water)
2 packages (8-serving size) or 4 packages (4-serving size) JELL-O® Brand Gelatin Dessert, any flavor

STIR boiling juice into gelatin in large bowl at least 3 minutes until completely dissolved. Pour into 13×9-inch pan.

REFRIGERATE 3 hours or until firm (does not stick to finger when touched). Dip bottom of pan in warm water about 15 seconds. Cut into decorative shapes with cookie cutters all the way through gelatin or cut into 1-inch squares. Lift from pan. *Makes about 24 pieces*

Note: *Recipe can be halved. Use 8- or 9-inch square pan.*

Preparation Time: 10 minutes
Refrigerating Time: 3 hours

Juice Up Your JELL-O

All-Time Favorites

Miniature Cheesecakes

Add a candle to each of these desserts for a quick birthday party treat.

> 1 package (11.1 ounces) JELL-O® No Bake Real Cheesecake
> 2 tablespoons sugar
> ⅓ cup butter or margarine, melted
> 1½ cups cold milk
> 2 squares BAKER'S® Semi-Sweet Baking Chocolate, melted (optional)

MIX crumbs from mix, sugar and butter thoroughly with fork in medium bowl until crumbs are well moistened. Press onto bottoms of 12 paper-lined or foil-lined muffin cups.

BEAT milk and filling mix with electric mixer on low speed until blended. Beat on medium speed 3 minutes. (Filling will be thick.) Spoon over crumb mixture in muffin cups. Drizzle with melted chocolate, if desired.

REFRIGERATE at least 1 hour or until ready to serve. Garnish as desired. *Makes 12 servings*

Preparation Time: 15 minutes
Refrigerating Time: 1 hour

Miniature Cheesecakes

Watergate Salad
(Pistachio Pineapple Delight)

1 package (4-serving size) JELL-O® Pistachio Flavor Instant
    Pudding & Pie Filling
1 can (20 ounces) crushed pineapple in juice, undrained
1 cup miniature marshmallows
½ cup chopped nuts
2 cups thawed COOL WHIP® Whipped Topping

STIR pudding mix, pineapple with juice, marshmallows and nuts in large bowl until well blended. Gently stir in whipped topping.

REFRIGERATE 1 hour or until ready to serve. Garnish as desired.

Makes 8 servings

Preparation Time: 10 minutes
Refrigerating Time: 1 hour

JELL-O® Fun Facts

Originally named Pistachio Pineapple Delight, this salad first surfaced in 1976, the year Pistachio Flavor Instant Pudding & Pie Filling was launched. This recipe doubles as an accompaniment for your favorite poultry dish or simply as a dessert and continues to be one of our most requested recipes.

Watergate Salad (Pistachio Pineapple Delight)

Southern Banana Pudding

A classic expression of Southern hospitality.

   1 package (4-serving size) JELL-O® Vanilla or Banana Cream Flavor
       Cook & Serve Pudding & Pie Filling *(not Instant)*
2½ cups milk
   2 egg yolks, well beaten
30 to 35 vanilla wafers
   2 large bananas, sliced
   2 egg whites
       Dash salt
¼ cup sugar

HEAT oven to 350°F.

STIR pudding mix into milk in medium saucepan. Add egg yolks. Stirring constantly, cook on medium heat until mixture comes to full boil. Remove from heat.

ARRANGE layer of cookies on bottom and up side of 1½-quart baking dish. Add layer of banana slices; top with ⅓ of the pudding. Repeat layers twice, ending with pudding.

BEAT egg whites and salt in medium bowl with electric mixer on high speed until foamy. Gradually add sugar, beating until stiff peaks form. Spoon meringue mixture lightly onto pudding, spreading to edge of dish to seal.

BAKE 10 to 15 minutes or until meringue is lightly browned. Serve warm or refrigerate until ready to serve.   *Makes 8 servings*

Preparation Time: 30 minutes
Baking Time: 15 minutes

Southern Banana Pudding

Chocolate Cherry Cheesecake

2 packages (21.4 ounces each) JELL-O® No Bake Cherry or
    Strawberry Topped Cheesecake
¼ cup sugar
¾ cup butter or margarine, melted
2½ cups cold milk
3 squares BAKER'S® Semi-Sweet Baking Chocolate, melted and
    cooled

STIR crust mixes, sugar, butter and 2 tablespoons water with fork in medium bowl until crumbs are well moistened. First, firmly press ½ of crumbs 2 inches up side of 9-inch springform pan. Press remaining crumbs firmly onto bottom, using measuring cup. Spoon 1 fruit pouch over crust.

POUR cold milk into medium mixing bowl. Add Filling Mixes. Beat with electric mixer on lowest speed until blended. Beat on medium speed 3 minutes. Filling will be thick. Immediately stir 1 cup cheesecake mixture into chocolate until blended. Spoon mixture over fruit in crust. Top with remaining fruit pouch.

REFRIGERATE 4 hours or until firm. To serve, run a small knife or spatula around side of pan to loosen crust; remove side of pan.

Makes 16 servings

Note: *Cheesecake can also be prepared in a 13×9-inch baking pan, pressing all of the crust firmly onto bottom of pan. Continue as directed.*

Preparation Time: 15 minutes plus refrigerating

Gelatin Poke Cake

This fun cake can be made with any one of the JELL-O® gelatin flavors.

> 1 package (2-layer size) white cake mix or cake mix with pudding in the mix
> 1 cup boiling water
> 1 package (4-serving size) JELL-O® Brand Gelatin Dessert, any flavor
> ½ cup cold water
> 1 tub (8 ounces) COOL WHIP® Whipped Topping, thawed

HEAT oven to 350°F.

PREPARE and bake cake mix as directed on package for 13×9-inch baking pan. Remove from oven. Cool cake in pan 15 minutes. Pierce cake with large fork at ½-inch intervals.

MEANWHILE, stir boiling water into gelatin in medium bowl at least 2 minutes until completely dissolved. Stir in cold water; carefully pour over cake. Refrigerate 3 hours.

FROST with whipped topping. Refrigerate at least 1 hour or until ready to serve. Decorate as desired.   *Makes 15 servings*

Preparation Time: 15 minutes
Baking Time: 35 minutes
Refrigerating Time: 4 hours

JELL-O® Fun Facts

This classic recipe can be made as cup cakes or a layer cake. Also, by simply changing the flavor of gelatin, you can tailor it to suit your favorite holiday. For example, red for Valentine's Day or orange for Halloween.

Creamy Vanilla Sauce

3½ cups cold milk, light cream or half-and-half
   1 package (4-serving size) JELL-O® Vanilla or French Vanilla Flavor
      Instant Pudding & Pie Filling

POUR milk into bowl. Add pudding mix. Beat with wire whisk
2 minutes. Cover.

REFRIGERATE until ready to serve. Serve over your favorite fruits or
cake. Garnish as desired. *Makes 3½ cups*

Creamy Citrus Sauce: *Add 2 teaspoons grated orange peel with pudding
mix.*

Preparation Time: 5 minutes

Frozen Cheesecake Pie

   1 package (21.4 ounces) JELL-O® No Bake Cherry or Strawberry
      Topped Cheesecake
   2 tablespoons sugar
   ⅓ cup butter or margarine, melted
1½ cups cold milk
   1 tub (8 ounces) COOL WHIP® Whipped Topping, thawed

MIX crumbs, sugar and butter thoroughly with fork in 9-inch pie plate
until crumbs are well moistened. Press firmly against side of plate first,
using finger or large spoon to shape edge. Press remaining crumbs
firmly onto bottom using measuring cup.

BEAT milk and filling mix in medium bowl with electric mixer on low
speed until blended. Beat on medium speed 3 minutes. (Filling will be
thick.) Stir in whipped topping until smooth. Swirl fruit topping into
mixture with spatula. Spoon into crust.

FREEZE 6 hours or overnight until firm. Let stand at room
temperature or in refrigerator 15 minutes or until pie can be cut easily.
Makes 8 servings

Preparation Time: 15 minutes
Freezing Time: 6 hours

Creamy Vanilla Sauce

Double Chocolate Bread Pudding

The queen of comfort foods!

> **5 cups milk**
> **2 packages (4-serving size) JELL-O® Chocolate Fudge Flavor Cook**
>   **& Serve Pudding & Pie Filling** *(not Instant)*
> **5 cups cubed French bread**
> **1 cup BAKER'S® Semi-Sweet Real Chocolate Chips**

HEAT oven to 350°F.

POUR milk into large bowl. Add pudding mixes. Beat with wire whisk 1 minute. Stir in bread. Pour pudding mixture into 13×9-inch baking dish. Sprinkle evenly with chocolate chips.

BAKE 45 minutes or until mixture comes to boil. Remove from oven. Let stand 10 minutes. Serve warm.   *Makes 15 servings*

Preparation Time: 15 minutes
Baking Time: 45 minutes

JELL-O® Fun Facts

A recipe for bread pudding appeared in American cookbooks as early as 1796. It has always been a favorite in the South and has re-emerged nationwide as a welcome homey "comfort" food.

All-American Trifle

A summer trifle perfect for any patriotic holiday.

4 cups boiling water
1 package (8-serving size) or 2 packages (4-serving size) JELL-O®
   Brand Gelatin Dessert, any red flavor
1 package (8-serving size) or 2 packages (4-serving size) JELL-O®
   Brand Berry Blue Flavor Gelatin Dessert
2 cups cold water
4 cups cubed pound cake
2 cups sliced strawberries
1 tub (8 ounces) COOL WHIP® Whipped Topping, thawed

STIR 2 cups of the boiling water into each flavor of gelatin in separate bowls at least 2 minutes until completely dissolved. Stir 1 cup cold water into each bowl. Pour into separate 13×9-inch pans. Refrigerate 3 hours until firm. Cut each pan into ½-inch cubes.

PLACE red gelatin cubes in 3½-quart bowl or trifle bowl. Layer with cake cubes, strawberries and ½ of the whipped topping. Cover with blue gelatin cubes. Garnish with remaining whipped topping.

REFRIGERATE at least 1 hour or until ready to serve.

Makes 16 servings

Preparation Time: 20 minutes
Refrigerating Time: 4 hours

Luscious Pies

Cookies & Creme Café Pie

1 package (12.6 ounces) JELL-O® No Bake Cookies & Creme
   Dessert
⅓ cup butter or margarine, melted
1⅓ cups cold milk
¼ cup GENERAL FOODS INTERNATIONAL COFFEE®, Suisse
   Mocha Flavor, Vanilla Café Flavor or Irish Cream Café Flavor

STIR crust mix and butter thoroughly with spoon in medium bowl until crumbs are well moistened. Press onto bottom and up side of 9-inch pie plate.

POUR cold milk into large bowl. Add filling mix and coffee. Beat with electric mixer on low speed 30 seconds. Beat on high speed 3 minutes. **Do not underbeat.**

RESERVE ½ cup of the crushed cookies. Gently stir remaining crushed cookies into filling until well blended. Spoon mixture into prepared pie crust. Top with reserved cookies. Refrigerate 4 hours or until firm or freeze 2 hours to serve frozen.   *Makes 8 servings*

Preparation Time: 15 minutes plus refrigerating

Cookies & Creme Café Pie

No Bake Cappuccino Cheesecake

The flavors of coffee and cinnamon add spark to this sophisticated dessert.

> 1 package (11.1 ounces) JELL-O® No Bake Real Cheesecake
> 2 tablespoons sugar
> ⅓ cup butter or margarine, melted
> 2 teaspoons MAXWELL HOUSE® Instant Coffee
> 1½ cups cold milk
> ¼ teaspoon ground cinnamon

MIX crumbs, sugar and butter thoroughly with fork in 9-inch pie plate until crumbs are well moistened. Press firmly against side of pie plate first, using finger or large spoon to shape edge. Press remaining crumbs firmly onto bottom using measuring cup.

DISSOLVE coffee in milk. Beat milk mixture, filling mix and cinnamon with electric mixer on low speed until blended. Beat on medium speed 3 minutes. (Filling will be thick.) Spoon into crust. Garnish with crushed chocolate sandwich cookies, if desired.

REFRIGERATE at least 1 hour.   *Makes 8 servings*

Preparation Time: 15 minutes
Refrigerating Time: 1 hour

JELL-O® Fun Facts

If you are having a crowd, this is a perfect recipe to make. Just double all the ingredients and use a 13×9-inch pan. For an extra special garnish, serve each square with a spoonful of COOL WHIP Whipped topping and a chocolate covered coffee bean.

No Bake Cappuccino Cheesecake

COOL 'N EASY® Pie

Ten minutes in the morning—luscious strawberry pie in the evening!

⅔ cup boiling water
1 package (4-serving size) JELL-O® Brand Gelatin, any flavor
½ cup cold juice, any flavor
  Ice cubes
1 tub (8 ounces) COOL WHIP® Whipped Topping, thawed
1 prepared graham cracker crumb crust (6 ounces)
  Assorted fruit (optional)

STIR boiling water into gelatin in large bowl 2 minutes or until completely dissolved. Mix cold juice and ice to make 1 cup. Add to gelatin, stirring until slightly thickened. Remove any remaining ice.

STIR in whipped topping with wire whisk until smooth. Refrigerate 10 to 15 minutes or until mixture is very thick and will mound. Spoon into crust.

REFRIGERATE 4 hours or until firm. Just before serving, garnish with fruit and additional whipped topping, if desired. Store leftover pie in refrigerator.

Makes 8 servings

JELL-O® Fun Facts

This refreshing pie, which is a mixture of gelatin and whipped topping, can be easily transformed into any flavor by using different combinations of JELL-O gelatin, fruit and juice.

COOL 'N EASY® Pie

Juicy Triple Berry Pie

3 cups assorted berries
1 graham cracker crumb or shortbread pie crust (6 ounces)
½ cup sugar
2 tablespoons cornstarch
1½ cups orange or orange strawberry banana juice
1 package (4-serving size) JELL-O® Brand Gelatin, any red flavor

ARRANGE berries in crust.

MIX sugar and cornstarch in medium saucepan. Gradually stir in juice until smooth. Stirring constantly, cook over medium heat until mixture comes to a boil; boil 1 minute. Remove from heat. Stir in gelatin until completely dissolved. Cool to room temperature; pour into crust.

REFRIGERATE 3 hours or until firm. Garnish with COOL WHIP® Whipped Topping, if desired. Store leftover pie in refrigerator.

Makes 8 servings

Preparation Time: 20 minutes
Refrigerating Time: 3 hours

Juice Up Your JELL-O

JELL-O® Fun Facts

For an interesting flavor combination, use JELL-O Lemon Flavor Gelatin in place of red gelatin and 1½ cups fresh blueberries in place of strawberries.

5-Minute Double Layer Pie

1¼ cups cold milk
2 packages (4-serving size each) JELL-O® Instant Pudding & Pie Filling, Chocolate Flavor, Lemon Flavor or other flavor
1 tub (8 ounces) COOL WHIP® Whipped Topping, thawed, divided
1 prepared graham cracker crumb crust or chocolate pie crust (6 ounces or 9 inches)

BEAT milk, pudding mixes and ½ of the whipped topping in medium bowl with wire whisk 1 minute (mixture will be thick). Spread in crust.

SPREAD remaining whipped topping over pudding layer in crust. Refrigerate until ready to serve.   *Makes 8 servings*

Preparation Time: 5 minutes

Ice Cream Pudding Pie

1 cup cold milk
1 cup ice cream (any flavor), softened
1 package (4-serving size) JELL-O® Instant Pudding & Pie Filling, any flavor
1 prepared graham cracker crumb crust (6 ounces)

MIX milk and ice cream in large bowl. Add pudding mix. Beat with electric mixer on lowest speed 1 minute. Pour immediately into crust.

REFRIGERATE 2 hours or until set.   *Makes 8 servings*

Preparation Time: 10 minutes
Refrigerating Time: 2 hours

Frozen Banana Split Pie

The family will go nuts over this ice cream parlor dessert!

1½ **bananas, sliced**
1 **prepared graham cracker crumb crust (6 ounces)**
2 **cups cold milk**
1 **package (4-serving size) JELL-O® Vanilla or Banana Cream Flavor**
    Instant Pudding & Pie Filling
1 **tub (8 ounces) COOL WHIP® Whipped Topping, thawed**
    Chocolate, strawberry and pineapple dessert toppings
    Additional banana slices
    Chopped nuts

ARRANGE banana slices on bottom of crust; set aside.

POUR milk into large bowl. Add pudding mix. Beat with wire whisk 1 minute. Gently stir in 2 cups of the whipped topping. Spread over banana slices.

FREEZE 6 hours or until firm. Let stand at room temperature or in refrigerator 15 minutes or until pie can be cut easily. Top with dessert toppings, remaining whipped topping, banana slices and nuts.

Makes 8 servings

Preparation Time: 15 minutes
Freezing Time: 6 hours

Fun Facts

A great way to have fun with this pie is to slice up the pie and serve buffet style. Set out all different kinds of ice cream candy toppings and let everyone individualize their own slice.

Frozen Banana Split Pie

Key Lime Pie

Taste this cool summertime treat.

1¾ cups boiling water
1 package (8-serving size) or 2 packages (4-serving size) JELL-O®
    Brand Lime Flavor Gelatin Dessert
2 teaspoons grated lime peel
¼ cup lime juice
1 pint (2 cups) vanilla ice cream, softened
1 prepared graham cracker crumb crust (6 ounces)

STIR boiling water into gelatin in large bowl at least 2 minutes until completely dissolved. Stir in lime peel and juice.

STIR in ice cream until melted and smooth. Refrigerate 15 to 20 minutes or until mixture is very thick and will mound. Spoon into crust.

REFRIGERATE 2 hours or until firm. Garnish as desired.

Makes 8 servings

Preparation Time: 15 minutes
Refrigerating Time: 2½ hours

Key lime pie is typically made with small tart limes grown in Florida, not generally available in the rest of the U.S. This recipe is a quick and easy adaptation.

Key Lime Pie

Sensational Desserts

Peanut Butter Loaf

1 package (16.1 ounces) JELL-O® No Bake Peanut Butter Cup
    Dessert
⅓ cup butter or margarine, melted
1⅓ cups cold milk

PLACE topping pouch in large bowl of boiling water; set aside. Line
9×5-inch loaf pan with foil. Stir crust mix and butter with fork in
medium bowl until crumbs are well moistened. Press ½ of crumbs
firmly onto bottom of prepared pan; reserve remaining crumbs.

POUR cold milk into medium mixing bowl. Add filling mix and peanut
butter. Beat with electric mixer on lowest speed until blended. Beat on
high speed 3 minutes. **Do not underbeat.** Spoon ½ of filling mixture
over crust in pan.

REMOVE pouch from water. Shake vigorously 60 seconds until topping
is no longer lumpy. Squeeze ½ of topping over filling in pan. Repeat
layers with remaining crumbs and filling. Freeze 4 hours or overnight.
To serve, lift from pan to cutting board and remove foil. Let stand at
room temperature 10 minutes for easier slicing. Stand remaining
topping pouch in boiling water to soften. Drizzle each slice with topping.

Makes 8 to 10 servings

Preparation Time: 15 minutes
Freezing Time: 4 hours

Peanut Butter Loaf

Pastel Swirl Dessert

A lovely dessert suitable for a shower, luncheon or any occasion!

>   1 package (3 ounces) ladyfingers, split
> 1⅓ cups boiling water
>   2 packages (4-serving size) JELL-O® Brand Gelatin Dessert,
>   any 2 different flavors
>   1 cup cold water
>   Ice cubes
>   1 tub (12 ounces) COOL WHIP® Whipped Topping, thawed, divided

TRIM about 1 inch off 1 end of each ladyfinger; reserve trimmed ends. Place ladyfingers, cut ends down, around side of 9-inch springform pan.* Place trimmed ends on bottom of pan.

STIR ⅔ cup of the boiling water into each package of gelatin in separate medium bowls at least 2 minutes until completely dissolved. Mix cold water and ice cubes to make 2½ cups. Stir ½ of the ice water into each bowl until gelatin is slightly thickened. Remove any remaining ice.

GENTLY stir ½ of the whipped topping with wire whisk into each gelatin mixture until smooth. Refrigerate 20 to 30 minutes or until mixtures are very thick and will mound. Spoon mixtures alternately into prepared pan. Swirl with knife to marbleize.

REFRIGERATE 4 hours or until firm. Remove side of pan before slicing.   *Makes 16 servings*

*To prepare in 13×9-inch pan, do not trim ladyfingers. Line bottom of pan with ladyfingers. Continue as directed.

Preparation Time: 30 minutes
Refrigerating Time: 4½ hours

Pastel Swirl Dessert

White Chocolate Cheesecake

A truly luxurious dessert with a rich, silky texture.

    1 package (11.1 ounces) JELL-O® No Bake Real Cheesecake
    ⅓ cup butter or margarine, melted
    2 tablespoons sugar
    1½ cups cold milk
    1 package (6 squares) BAKER'S® Premium White Baking Chocolate
       Squares, melted
    2 squares BAKER'S® Semi-Sweet Baking Chocolate, melted
       (optional)

MIX crumbs, butter and sugar thoroughly with fork in 9-inch pie plate until crumbs are well moistened. Press firmly against side of pie plate first, using finger or large spoon to shape edge. Press remaining crumbs firmly onto bottom of pie plate using measuring cup.

BEAT milk and filling mix with electric mixer on low speed until blended. Beat on medium speed 3 minutes. (Filling will be thick.) Reserve about 3 tablespoons melted white chocolate for garnish, if desired. Stir remaining melted white chocolate into filling mixture. Spoon into crust. Drizzle with reserved melted white chocolate and melted semi-sweet chocolate, if desired.

REFRIGERATE at least 1 hour, if desired.   *Makes 8 servings*

Preparation Time: 15 minutes
Refrigerating Time: 1 hour

*Take the mystery out of making cheesecake
with this recipe made extra simple with
JELL-O No Bake Cheesecake.*

White Chocolate Cheesecake

Tropical Terrine

A slice of this will magically transport you to a beach in the Caribbean.

   1 package (3 ounces) ladyfingers, split, divided
1½ cups boiling water
   1 package (8-serving size) or 2 packages (4-serving size) JELL-O®
      Brand Orange Flavor Sugar Free Low Calorie Gelatin Dessert
   1 can (8 ounces) crushed pineapple in juice, undrained
   1 cup cold water
   2 cups thawed COOL WHIP LITE® Whipped Topping
   1 can (11 ounces) mandarin orange segments, drained
     Additional thawed COOL WHIP LITE® Whipped Topping
     Kiwi slices
     Star fruit slices
     Pineapple leaves

LINE bottom and sides of 9×5-inch loaf pan with plastic wrap. Add enough ladyfingers, cut sides in, to fit evenly along all sides of pan.

STIR boiling water into gelatin in large bowl 2 minutes or until completely dissolved. Stir in pineapple with juice and cold water. Refrigerate 1¼ hours or until slightly thickened (consistency of unbeaten egg whites). Gently stir in 2 cups whipped topping and oranges. Spoon into prepared pan. Arrange remaining ladyfingers, cut sides down, evenly on top of gelatin mixture.

REFRIGERATE 3 hours or until firm. Place serving plate on top of pan. Invert, holding pan and plate together; shake gently to loosen. Carefully remove pan and plastic wrap. Garnish with additional whipped topping, fruit and pineapple leaves.   *Makes 12 servings*

Preparation Time: 30 minutes
Refrigerating Time: 4½ hours

COOL TIPS: *If you put a dab of shortening in the corners of the loaf pan, the plastic wrap will adhere to the pan more smoothly and easily. To keep its shape, leftover dessert can be returned to the loaf pan and refrigerated.*

JELL-O® *Frozen No Bake Peanut Butter Cups*

1 package (16.1 ounces) JELL-O® No Bake Peanut Butter Cup
   Dessert
⅓ cup melted margarine
1⅓ cups cold milk

PLACE topping pouch in large bowl of boiling water; set aside.

PREPARE crust mix as directed on package in medium bowl. Press onto bottoms of 12 to 15 foil-cup-lined muffin cups (about 1 heaping tablespoon per muffin cup).

PREPARE filling mix as directed on package in deep, medium bowl. Divide filling among muffin cups. Remove pouch from water. Knead pouch 60 seconds until fluid and no longer lumpy. Squeeze topping equally over cups.

FREEZE 2 hours or until firm. Store, covered, in freezer up to 2 weeks.

Makes 12 to 15 cups

JELL-O® Frozen No Bake Cookies & Creme Cups: *Prepare JELL-O® No Bake Cookies & Creme Dessert as directed on package, pressing prepared crust mix onto bottoms of 12 foil-cup-lined muffin cups. Divide prepared filling mixture among cups. Top with reserved cookies. Freeze and store as directed above.*

Preparation Time: 15 minutes plus freezing

Easy Eclair Dessert

This terrific dessert is a great crowd pleaser.

> 27 whole graham crackers, halved
> 3 cups cold milk
> 2 packages (4-serving size) JELL-O® Vanilla Flavor Instant Pudding & Pie Filling
> 1 tub (12 ounces) COOL WHIP® Whipped Topping, thawed
> 1 container (16 ounces) ready-to-spread chocolate fudge frosting
> Strawberries

ARRANGE ⅓ of the crackers on bottom of 13×9-inch baking pan, breaking crackers to fit, if necessary.

POUR milk into large bowl. Add pudding mixes. Beat with wire whisk 2 minutes. Gently stir in whipped topping. Spread ½ of the pudding mixture·over crackers. Place ½ of the remaining crackers over pudding; top with remaining pudding mixture and crackers.

REMOVE top and foil from frosting container. Microwave frosting in container on HIGH 1 minute or until pourable. Spread evenly over crackers.

REFRIGERATE 4 hours or overnight. Cut into squares to serve. Garnish with strawberries. *Makes 18 servings*

Preparation Time: 20 minutes
Refrigerating Time: 4 hours

JELL-O Pudding is the perfect ingredient for making easy homemade desserts. To make this already delicious dessert even more decadent, try substituting chocolate graham crackers and chocolate pudding for the ones used above. This is any chocoholic's dream!

Easy Eclair Dessert

Holiday Specialties

Tropical Cake Squares

1½ cups boiling water
   1 package (8-serving size) or 2 packages (4-serving size each)
      JELL-O® Brand Orange Flavor Gelatin
   2 cups cold pineapple orange juice or orange juice
   1 package (12 ounces) pound cake, cut into 10 to 12 slices
   1 package (8 ounces) PHILADELPHIA® Cream Cheese, softened
¼ cup sugar
   1 tub (8 ounces) COOL WHIP® Whipped Topping, thawed
   2 cans (15¼ ounces each) fruit cocktail, drained

STIR boiling water into gelatin in large bowl at least 2 minutes until completely dissolved. Stir in cold juice. Refrigerate about 1½ hours or until thickened (spoon drawn through leaved definite impression). Meanwhile, line 13×9-inch pan with pound cake slices, filling any holes with cake pieces.

BEAT cream cheese and sugar in large bowl until smooth. Gently stir in whipped topping. Spread evenly over crust. Top with fruit. Spoon thickened gelatin over cream cheese layer and fruit.

REFRIGERATE 3 hours or until firm.   *Makes 15 servings*

Preparation Time: 15 minutes
Refrigerating Time: 4½ hours

Tropical Cake Square

Sparkling Dessert

1½ cups boiling water
1 package (8-serving size) or 2 packages (4-serving size) JELL-O®
  Brand Sparkling White Grape or Lemon Flavor Gelatin Dessert
2½ cups cold club soda or seltzer
1 cup sliced strawberries

STIR boiling water into gelatin in large bowl at least 2 minutes until completely dissolved. Refrigerate 15 minutes. Stir in cold club soda. Refrigerate 25 minutes or until slightly thickened.

SET aside ¾ cup thickened gelatin in medium bowl. Gently stir strawberries into remaining gelatin. Spon into champagne glasses, dessert dishes or 2-quart bowl. Beat reserved gelatin with electric mixer or high speed until fluffy and about double in volume. Spoon over gelatin in glasses or bowl. Cover.

REFRIGERATE 3 hours or until firm.   *Makes 8 to 10 servings*

Note: To prepare with champagne, use 1 cup cold champagne and 1½ cups cold club soda.

Preparation Time: 15 minutes
Refrigerating Time: 3¾ hours

Choose the best container for efficiency when making this recipe. Metal bowls chill more quickly than glass or plastic bowls so your gelatin will be firm in less time.

Sparkling Dessert

Graveyard Pudding Dessert

Even the ghosts will go for this!

3½ cups cold milk
  2 packages (4-serving size) JELL-O® Chocolate Flavor Instant
      Pudding & Pie Filling
  1 tub (12 ounces) COOL WHIP® Whipped Topping, thawed
  1 package (16 ounces) chocolate sandwich cookies, crushed
      Decorations: assorted rectangular-shaped sandwich cookies,
        decorator icings, candy corn and pumpkins

POUR milk into large bowl. Add pudding mixes. Beat with wire whisk or electric mixer on lowest speed 2 minutes or until blended. Gently stir in whipped topping and ½ of the crushed cookies. Spoon into 13×9-inch dish. Sprinkle with remaining crushed cookies.

REFRIGERATE 1 hour or until ready to serve. Decorate rectangular-shaped sandwich cookies with icings to make "tombstones." Stand tombstones on top of dessert with candies to resemble a graveyard.

Makes 15 servings

Preparation Time: 15 minutes
Refrigerating Time: 1 hour

JELL-O® Fun Facts

This recipe is a great one to remember when you are the person in charge of the school or team snack. It can easily be changed into a soccer or football field, hockey rink or any desired theme. Prepare as above and just garnish appropriately.

Graveyard Pudding Dessert

Ghoulish Punch

2 cups boiling water
1 package (8-serving size) or 2 packages (4-serving size) JELL-O®
    Brand Lime Flavor Gelatin Dessert
2 cups cold orange juice
1 liter cold seltzer
    Ice cubes
1 pint (2 cups) orange sherbet, slightly softened
1 orange, thinly sliced
1 lime, thinly sliced

STIR boiling water into gelatin in large bowl at least 2 minutes until completely dissolved. Stir in cold juice. Cool to room temperature.

JUST before serving, pour gelatin mixture into punch bowl. Add cold seltzer and ice cubes. Place scoops of sherbet and fruit slices in punch.

Makes 10 servings

Preparation Time: 15 minutes

JELL-O Gelatin with its wide variety of fruit flavors makes an excellent base for easy and delicious drinks for a crowd.

Cranberry Apple Pie

Chopped apple and walnuts add delightful crunch to this irresistible pie suitable for any holiday gathering.

2 cups boiling water
1 package (8-serving size) or 2 packages (4-serving size) JELL-O®
 Brand Cranberry Flavor Gelatin Dessert, or any red flavor
½ cup cold water
½ teaspoon ground cinnamon
⅛ teaspoon ground cloves
½ package (4 ounces) PHILADELPHIA® Cream Cheese, softened
¼ cup sugar
½ cup thawed COOL WHIP® Whipped Topping
1 prepared graham cracker crumb crust (6 ounces)
1 medium apple, chopped
½ cup chopped walnuts

STIR boiling water into gelatin in large bowl at least 2 minutes until completely dissolved. Stir in cold water and spices. Refrigerate about 1½ hours or until thickened (spoon drawn through leaves definite impression).

MEANWHILE, mix cream cheese and sugar in medium bowl with wire whisk until smooth. Gently stir in whipped topping. Spread onto bottom of crust. Refrigerate.

STIR apples and walnuts into thickened gelatin. Refrigerate 10 to 15 minutes or until mixture is very thick and will mound. Spoon over cream cheese layer.

REFRIGERATE 4 hours or until firm.   *Makes 8 servings*

Preparation Time: 20 minutes
Refrigerating Time: 5¾ hours

Double Layer Pumpkin Pie

It just wouldn't be Thanksgiving without this pie.

- ½ package (4 ounces) PHILADELPHIA® Cream Cheese, cubed, softened
- 1 tablespoon half-and-half or milk
- 1 tablespoon sugar
- 1 tub (8 ounces) COOL WHIP® Whipped Topping, thawed
- 1 prepared graham cracker crumb crust (6 ounces)
- 1 cup cold half-and-half or milk
- 2 packages (4-serving size) JELL-O® Vanilla Flavor Instant Pudding & Pie Filling
- 1 can (16 ounces) pumpkin
- 1 teaspoon ground cinnamon
- ½ teaspoon ground ginger
- ¼ teaspoon ground cloves

BEAT cream cheese, 1 tablespoon half-and-half and sugar in large bowl with wire whisk until smooth. Gently stir in 1½ cups whipped topping. Spread onto bottom of crust.

POUR 1 cup half-and-half into bowl. Add pudding mixes. Beat with wire whisk 1 minute. (Mixture will be thick.) Stir in pumpkin and spices with wire whisk until well blended. Spread over cream cheese layer.

REFRIGERATE 4 hours or until set. Garnish with remaining whipped topping and sprinkle with additional cinnamon.   *Makes 8 servings*

Double Layer Chocolate Pie: *Omit pumpkin and spices and increase half-and-half to 1½ cups. Prepare recipe as directed, substituting JELL-O Chocolate Flavor Instant Pudding for vanilla pudding.*

Preparation Time: 15 minutes
Refrigerating Time: 4 hours

Double Layer Pumpkin Pie

Quick-and-Easy Holiday Trifle

A festive trifle that takes but a trifling twenty minutes to make.

> **3 cups cold milk**
> **2 packages (4-serving size) JELL-O® Vanilla Flavor Instant Pudding & Pie Filling**
> **1 tub (8 ounces) COOL WHIP® Whipped Topping, thawed**
> **1 package (12 ounces) pound cake, cut into ½-inch cubes**
> **¼ cup orange juice**
> **2 cups sliced strawberries**

POUR milk into large bowl. Add pudding mixes. Beat with wire whisk 1 minute. Gently stir in 2 cups of the whipped topping.

ARRANGE ½ of the cake cubes in 3½-quart serving bowl. Drizzle with ½ of the orange juice. Spoon ½ of the pudding mixture over cake cubes. Top with strawberries. Layer with remaining cake cubes, orange juice and pudding mixture.

REFRIGERATE until ready to serve. Top with remaining whipped topping and garnish as desired. *Makes 12 servings*

Preparation Time: 20 minutes
Refrigerating Time: 1 hour

Quick-and-Easy Holiday Trifle

Layered Cranberry Cheesecake

Tangy cranberries and crunchy walnuts make this festive cheesecake extra special.

> 1 package (11.1 ounces) JELL-O® No Bake Real Cheesecake
> 2 tablespoons sugar
> ⅓ cup butter or margarine, melted
> 1½ cups cold milk
> ½ cup whole berry cranberry sauce
> ¼ cup chopped walnuts, toasted

MIX crumbs, sugar and butter thoroughly with fork in small bowl until crumbs are well moistened. Press firmly onto bottom of foil-lined 9-inch square pan.

BEAT milk and filling mix with electric mixer on low speed until well blended. Beat on medium speed 3 minutes. (Filling will be thick.) Spoon ½ of the filling over crust. Cover with cranberry sauce and walnuts. Top with remaining filling.

REFRIGERATE at least 1 hour. Garnish as desired.

Makes 9 servings

Preparation Time: 15 minutes
Refrigerating Time: 1 hour

Cheesecake dates back to the Roman Empire days and still remains one of the most popular desserts of all times.

JELL-O®
BRAND

Celebrating 100 Years

JELL-O®

BRAND

Celebrating 100 Years

Shimmering Molds

Cucumber Sour Cream Mold

Complement poached salmon or shrimp with this refreshingly cool molded salad.

- 1½ **cups boiling water**
- 1 **package (8-serving size) or 2 packages (4-serving size) JELL-O Brand Lime Flavor Gelatin Dessert**
- ¼ **teaspoon salt**
- 1½ **cups cold water**
- 1 **tablespoon lemon juice**
- ½ **cup MIRACLE WHIP Salad Dressing**
- ½ **cup BREAKSTONE'S Sour Cream**
- 1½ **cups chopped seeded, peeled cucumber**
- 2 **tablespoons minced onion**
- 1 **teaspoon dill weed**

STIR boiling water into gelatin and salt in large bowl at least 2 minutes until completely dissolved. Stir in cold water and lemon juice. Refrigerate about 1¼ hours or until slightly thickened (consistency of unbeaten egg whites).

MIX salad dressing and sour cream in small bowl until well blended. Stir into thickened gelatin. Refrigerate about 15 minutes or until thickened (spoon drawn through leaves definite impression). Stir in cucumbers, onion and dill weed. Pour into 5-cup mold.

REFRIGERATE 4 hours or until firm. Unmold. Garnish as desired.

Makes 10 servings

Preparation Time: 15 minutes
Refrigerating Time: 5½ hours

83

Top to bottom: Cranberry Cream Cheese Mold (page 84), Sunset Fruit Salad (page 94), White Sangria Splash (page 85), Cucumber Sour Cream Mold

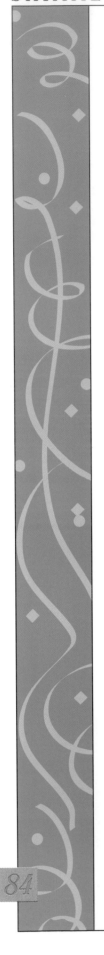

Cranberry Cream Cheese Mold

Piquant cranberry flavor is one of the hits of the 1990's. Now you no longer have to save it just for the Thanksgiving holiday.

Add sparkle to your festive buffet with this dramatic double-layer fruit mold.

1½ **cups boiling water**
  1 **package (8-serving size) or 2 packages (4-serving size) JELL-O Brand Cranberry Flavor Gelatin Dessert, or any red flavor**
1½ **cups cold water**
  ½ **teaspoon ground cinnamon**
  1 **medium apple, chopped**
  1 **cup whole berry cranberry sauce**
  1 **package (8 ounces) PHILADELPHIA BRAND Cream Cheese, softened**

STIR boiling water into gelatin in large bowl at least 2 minutes until completely dissolved. Stir in cold water and cinnamon. Reserve 1 cup gelatin at room temperature. Refrigerate remaining gelatin about 1½ hours or until thickened (spoon drawn through leaves definite impression).

STIR apple and cranberry sauce into thickened gelatin. Spoon into 6-cup mold. Refrigerate about 30 minutes or until set but not firm (gelatin should stick to finger when touched and should mound).

STIR reserved 1 cup gelatin gradually into cream cheese in medium bowl with wire whisk until smooth. Pour over gelatin layer in mold.

REFRIGERATE 4 hours or until firm. Unmold. Garnish as desired.   *Makes 12 servings*

Note: *To prepare without cream cheese layer, omit cream cheese. Refrigerate all of the gelatin about 1½ hours or until thickened. Stir in apple and cranberry sauce. Pour into mold. Refrigerate.*

Preparation Time: 20 minutes
Refrigerating Time: 6 hours

White Sangria Splash

Wine adds the right touch to this fruity dessert.

1 cup dry white wine
**1 package (8-serving size) or 2 packages
    (4-serving size) JELL-O Brand Lemon
    Flavor Sugar Free Low Calorie Gelatin
    Dessert or JELL-O Brand Lemon Flavor
    Gelatin Dessert**
3 cups cold seltzer or club soda
1 tablespoon lime juice
1 tablespoon orange juice or orange liqueur
3 cups seedless grapes, divided
1 cup sliced strawberries
1 cup whole small strawberries

Gelatin desserts made with wine have long been favorites for elegant entertaining. They are easy to make and impressive to serve. JELL-O gelatin can even trap the bubbles from champagne.

BRING wine to boil in small saucepan. Stir boiling wine into gelatin in medium bowl at least 2 minutes until completely dissolved. Stir in cold seltzer and lime and orange juices. Place bowl of gelatin in larger bowl of ice and water. Let stand about 10 minutes or until thickened (spoon drawn through leaves definite impression), stirring occasionally.

STIR in 1 cup of the grapes and the sliced strawberries. Pour into 6-cup mold.

REFRIGERATE 4 hours or until firm. Unmold. Garnish with remaining grapes and whole strawberries.   *Makes 12 servings*

 Nutrition Information Per Serving (using JELL-O Brand Lemon Flavor Sugar Free Low Calorie Gelatin Dessert and orange juice): *60 calories, 0g fat, 0mg cholesterol, 55mg sodium, 9g carbohydrate, 1g dietary fiber, 9g sugars, 1g protein, 35% daily value vitamin C*

Preparation Time: 15 minutes
Refrigerating Time: 4 hours

85

Gazpacho Salad

This jazzed-up variation on tomato aspic adopts the flavor and texture of the famous Spanish cold soup.

Enjoy the taste of Spain with this fat free tangy salad.

    1 cup diced tomato
  ½ cup diced peeled cucumber
  ¼ cup diced green pepper
    2 tablespoons diced red pepper
    2 tablespoons thinly sliced green onion
    2 tablespoons vinegar
  ¼ teaspoon pepper
  ⅛ teaspoon garlic powder (optional)
1½ cups tomato juice
    1 package (4-serving size) JELL-O Brand Lemon Flavor Sugar Free Low Calorie Gelatin Dessert or JELL-O Brand Lemon Flavor Gelatin Dessert
Crackers (optional)

MIX vegetables, vinegar, pepper and garlic powder in medium bowl; set aside. Bring tomato juice to boil in small saucepan. Stir into gelatin in large bowl at least 2 minutes until completely dissolved. Refrigerate about 1¼ hours or until slightly thickened (consistency of unbeaten egg whites).

STIR in vegetable mixture. Pour into 4-cup mold.

REFRIGERATE 3 hours or until firm. Unmold. Serve with crackers if desired. Garnish as desired.

Makes 6 servings

Nutrition Information Per Serving (using JELL-O Brand Lemon Flavor Sugar Free Low Calorie Gelatin Dessert and omitting crackers and garnish): *30 calories, 0g fat, 0mg cholesterol, 260mg sodium, 5g carbohydrate, less than 1g dietary fiber, 4g sugars, 2g protein, 15% daily value vitamin A, 50% daily value vitamin C*

Preparation Time: 20 minutes
Refrigerating Time: 4¼ hours

87

Gazpacho Salad

1911

Creamy Fruited Mold

Fluffy and delicious!

1 cup boiling water
1 package (4-serving size) JELL-O
    Brand Gelatin Dessert, any flavor
1 cup cold water or apple juice
2½ cups thawed COOL WHIP Whipped
    Topping
1 cup diced fruit

STIR boiling water into gelatin in medium bowl at least 2 minutes until completely dissolved. Stir in cold water. Refrigerate about 1¼ hours or until slightly thickened (consistency of unbeaten egg whites). Gently stir in whipped topping. Refrigerate about 15 minutes or until thickened (spoon drawn through leaves definite impression). Stir in fruit. Pour into 5-cup mold.

REFRIGERATE 4 hours or until firm. Unmold. Garnish as desired.

Makes 8 servings

Preparation Time: 15 minutes
Refrigerating Time: 5½ hours

89

Creamy Fruited Mold

Layered Pear Cream Cheese Mold

Carbonated beverages add pizzazz to molded gelatin salads. Club soda, fruit-flavored sparkling water, ginger ale or lemon-lime flavored drinks can be substituted for all or part of the cold water.

Guests will enjoy this beautiful emerald-topped mold flavored with a hint of ginger.

1 can (16 ounces) pear halves, undrained
1 package (8-serving size) or 2 packages (4-serving size) JELL-O Brand Lime Flavor Gelatin Dessert
1½ cups cold ginger ale or water
2 tablespoons lemon juice
1 package (8 ounces) PHILADELPHIA BRAND Cream Cheese, softened
¼ cup chopped pecans

DRAIN pears, reserving liquid. Dice pears; set aside. Add water to liquid to make 1½ cups; bring to boil in small saucepan.

STIR boiling liquid into gelatin in large bowl at least 2 minutes until completely dissolved. Stir in cold ginger ale and lemon juice. Reserve 2½ cups gelatin at room temperature. Pour remaining gelatin into 5-cup mold. Refrigerate about 30 minutes or until thickened (spoon drawn through leaves definite impression). Arrange about ½ cup of the diced pears in thickened gelatin in mold.

STIR reserved 2½ cups gelatin gradually into cream cheese in large bowl with wire whisk until smooth. Refrigerate about 30 minutes or until slightly thickened (consistency of unbeaten egg whites). Stir in remaining diced pears and pecans. Spoon over gelatin layer in mold.

REFRIGERATE 4 hours or until firm. Unmold. Garnish as desired.　　*Makes 10 servings*

Preparation Time: 30 minutes
Refrigerating Time: 5 hours

Layered Pear Cream Cheese Mold

Vegetable Trio Mold

2 cups boiling water
1 package (8-serving size) or
    2 packages
    (4-serving size) JELL-O Brand
    Lemon Flavor Gelatin Dessert
½ teaspoon salt
1½ cups cold water
3 tablespoons vinegar
1¼ cups grated carrots
½ cup KRAFT Mayo: Real Mayonnaise
    or MIRACLE WHIP Salad Dressing
1 cup shredded zucchini
¼ cup sliced green onions

STIR boiling water into gelatin and salt in large bowl at least 2 minutes until completely dissolved. Stir in cold water and vinegar. Reserve 2¾ cups gelatin at room temperature. Refrigerate remaining gelatin about 1 hour or until thickened (spoon drawn through leaves definite impression).

STIR carrots into thickened gelatin. Spoon into 5-cup mold. Refrigerate about 15 minutes or until set but not firm (gelatin should stick to finger when touched and should mound).

STIR 1 cup of the reserved gelatin into mayonnaise in medium bowl with wire whisk until smooth. Spoon over gelatin layer in mold. Refrigerate about 30 minutes or until set but not firm (gelatin should stick to finger when touched and should mound). Stir zucchini and green onions into remaining reserved gelatin. Spoon over gelatin layer in mold.

REFRIGERATE 3 hours or until firm. Unmold. Garnish as desired.

Makes 10 servings

Preparation Time: 30 minutes
Refrigerating Time: 4¾ hours

Vegetable Trio Mold

Sunset Fruit Salad

This recipe was first created in 1931, when molded gelatin salads were at the height of their popularity. At that time, almost one third of the salad recipes in the average cookbook were gelatin-based.

This spectacular fat free salad reflects the colors of the setting sun.

2 cups boiling water
1 package (4-serving size) JELL-O Brand Cranberry Flavor Sugar Free Low Calorie Gelatin Dessert or JELL-O Brand Cranberry Flavor Gelatin Dessert, or any red flavor
½ cup cold water
1 can (8 ounces) sliced peaches in juice, drained, chopped
1 package (4-serving size) JELL-O Brand Orange Flavor Sugar Free Low Calorie Gelatin Dessert or JELL-O Brand Orange Flavor Gelatin Dessert
1 can (8 ounces) crushed pineapple in juice, undrained

STIR 1 cup of the boiling water into cranberry gelatin in medium bowl at least 2 minutes until completely dissolved. Stir in cold water. Refrigerate about 45 minutes or until slightly thickened (consistency of unbeaten egg whites). Stir in peaches. Spoon into 5-cup mold. Refrigerate about 15 minutes or until set but not firm (gelatin should stick to finger when touched and should mound).

MEANWHILE, stir remaining 1 cup boiling water into orange gelatin in medium bowl at least 2 minutes until completely dissolved. Stir in pineapple with juice. Pour over gelatin layer in mold.

REFRIGERATE 4 hours or until firm. Unmold. Garnish as desired. *Makes 10 servings*

Nutrition Information Per Serving (using JELL-O Brand Cranberry and Orange Flavors Sugar Free Low Calorie Gelatin Dessert and omitting garnish): *30 calories, 0g fat, 0mg cholesterol, 60mg sodium, 6g carbohydrate, 0g dietary fiber, 7g sugars, 1g protein*

Preparation Time: 20 minutes
Refrigerating Time: 5 hours

Waldorf Salad

A delectable molded version of a salad classic.

> 2 cups boiling water
> 1 package (8-serving size) or 2 packages
>   (4-serving size) JELL-O Brand Lemon
>   Flavor Gelatin Dessert
> 1 cup cold water
> 1 tablespoon lemon juice
> ½ cup KRAFT Mayo: Real Mayonnaise or
>   MIRACLE WHIP Salad Dressing
> 1 medium red apple, diced
> ½ cup diced celery
> ¼ cup chopped walnuts
>   Salad greens (optional)

The original Waldorf salad was created in the 1890's at New York's Waldorf-Astoria Hotel. It consisted of apples, celery and mayonnaise and was served on lettuce. The walnuts were added to the recipe in later years.

STIR boiling water into gelatin in large bowl at least 2 minutes until completely dissolved. Stir in cold water and lemon juice. Refrigerate about 1½ hours or until thickened (spoon drawn through leaves definite impression). Gradually stir in mayonnaise with wire whisk. Stir in apple, celery and walnuts. Pour into 5-cup mold.

REFRIGERATE 4 hours or until firm. Unmold. Serve on salad greens, if desired.

Makes 10 servings

Preparation Time: 20 minutes
Refrigerating Time: 5½ hours

A 1908 ad offered a free set of six aluminum molds to JELL-O users. They were directed to buy a package of JELL-O gelatin for 10 cents to learn how to obtain the molds.

Snack Attacks

Pudding Chillers

After school is the perfect time for savoring these frozen pops.

> **2 cups cold milk**
> **1 package (4-serving size) JELL-O Instant Pudding & Pie Filling, any flavor**
> **6 (5-ounce) paper cups**

POUR milk into medium bowl. Add pudding mix. Beat with wire whisk 2 minutes. Spoon into cups. Insert wooden pop stick into each for a handle.

FREEZE 5 hours or overnight until firm. To remove pop from cup, place bottom of cup under warm running water for 15 seconds. Press firmly on bottom of cup to release pop. (Do not twist or pull pop stick.)
Makes 6 pops

Rocky Road: Use JELL-O Chocolate Flavor Instant Pudding & Pie Filling and stir in ½ cup miniature marshmallows and ¼ cup *each* BAKER'S Semi-Sweet Real Chocolate Chips and chopped peanuts.

Toffee Crunch: Use JELL-O Vanilla Flavor Instant Pudding & Pie Filling and stir in ½ cup chopped chocolate-covered toffee bars.

Cookies & Cream: Use JELL-O Vanilla Flavor Instant Pudding & Pie Filling and stir in ½ cup chopped chocolate sandwich cookies.

Preparation Time: 10 minutes
Freezing Time: 5 hours

Clockwise from top left: Rocky Road Pudding Chillers, Cookies & Cream Pudding Chillers, Pudding in a Cloud (page 105), JIGGLERS® (page 100), Creamy JIGGLERS® (page 100)

97

Refreshers

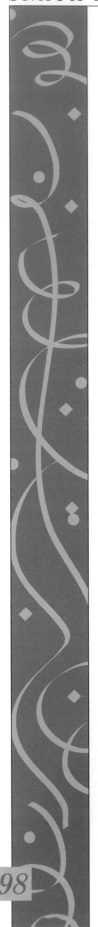

In 1991, the Smithsonian Institution held its first and only conference on JELL-O history, featuring such topics as American History is JELL-O History, JELL-O Food Wrestling, and The Dialectics of JELL-O in Peasant Culture.

1 cup boiling water
1 package (4-serving size) JELL-O Brand Gelatin Dessert, any flavor
1 cup cold beverage, such as seltzer, club soda, ginger ale, iced tea or lemon-lime carbonated beverage

STIR boiling water into gelatin in medium bowl at least 2 minutes until completely dissolved. Stir in cold beverage.

REFRIGERATE 4 hours or until firm. Cut into cubes and garnish as desired.   *Makes 4 servings*

Sugar Free Low Calorie Refreshers: Prepare recipe as directed above using any flavor JELL-O Brand Sugar Free Low Calorie Gelatin Dessert and 1 cup seltzer, club soda, diet ginger ale, diet iced tea or diet lemon-lime carbonated beverage.

Nutrition Information Per Serving (for Sugar Free Low Calorie Refreshers, omitting garnish): 10 calories, 0g fat, 0mg cholesterol, 90mg sodium, 0g carbohydrate, 0g dietary fiber, 0g sugars, 1g protein

Preparation Time: 5 minutes
Refrigerating Time: 4 hours

The first JELL-O flavors—strawberry, raspberry, orange and lemon—are still available today and are among the most popular flavors.

Refreshers

99

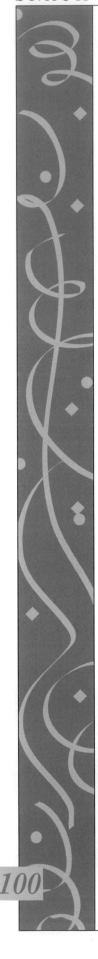

JIGGLERS®

Fabulous fun finger foods that kids adore!

Introduced in 1989, wiggly JELL-O JIGGLERS® is the most requested JELL-O recipe ever, according to the company's Consumer Response Center.

**2½ cups boiling water or boiling apple juice
    (Do not add cold water or cold juice.)
2 packages (8-serving size) or 4 packages
    (4-serving size) JELL-O Brand Gelatin
    Dessert, any flavor**

STIR boiling water or boiling juice into gelatin in large bowl at least 3 minutes until completely dissolved. Pour into 13×9-inch pan.

REFRIGERATE 3 hours or until firm. Dip bottom of pan in warm water about 15 seconds. Cut into decorative shapes with cookie cutters all the way through gelatin or cut into 1-inch squares. Lift from pan.   *Makes about 24 pieces*

Note: *Recipe can be halved. Use 8- or 9-inch square pan.*

Preparation Time: 10 minutes
Refrigerating Time: 3 hours

Creamy JIGGLERS®

**2½ cups boiling water
2 packages (8-serving size) or 4 packages
    (4-serving size) JELL-O Brand Gelatin
    Dessert, any flavor
1 cup cold milk
1 package (4-serving size) JELL-O Vanilla
    Flavor Instant Pudding & Pie Filling**

STIR boiling water into gelatin in large bowl at least 3 minutes until completely dissolved. Cool 30 minutes at room temperature.

POUR milk into medium bowl. Add pudding mix. Beat with wire whisk 1 minute. Quickly pour into gelatin. Stir with wire whisk until well blended. Pour into 13×9-inch pan.

REFRIGERATE 3 hours or until firm. Dip bottom of pan in warm water about 15 seconds. Cut into decorative shapes with cookie cutters all the way through gelatin or cut into 1-inch squares. Lift from pan. *Makes about 24 pieces*

Preparation Time: 15 minutes
Refrigerating Time: 3 hours

*S*trawberry Sorbet

Full of fruit flavor, this refreshing sorbet will melt in your mouth.

   1 package (10 ounces) frozen strawberries in syrup, thawed
   1 cup cold water
   2 cups boiling water
   1 package (4-serving size) JELL-O Brand Strawberry Flavor
       Gelatin Dessert
   ¾ cup sugar

PLACE strawberries and cold water in blender container; cover. Blend on high speed until smooth.

STIR boiling water into gelatin and sugar in large bowl at least 2 minutes until completely dissolved. Stir in strawberry mixture. Pour into 9-inch square pan.

FREEZE about 1 hour or until ice crystals form 1 inch around edges. Spoon into blender container; cover. Blend on high speed about 30 seconds or until smooth. Return to pan.

FREEZE 6 hours or overnight until firm. Scoop into dessert dishes.
Makes 10 servings

Preparation Time: 15 minutes
Freezing Time: 7 hours

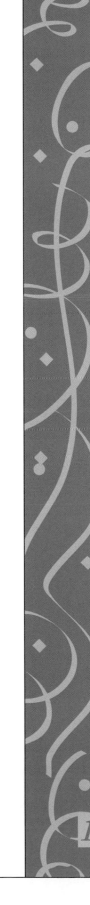

Yogurt Fluff

JELL-O gelatin has always been naturally fat free and pairing it with low fat yogurt makes a delightful combination.

Versatile yogurt adds creamy smoothness to this ever-so-simple low fat treat.

¾ **cup boiling water**
1 **package (4-serving size) JELL-O Brand Sugar Free Low Calorie Gelatin Dessert or JELL-O Brand Gelatin Dessert, any flavor**
½ **cup cold water or fruit juice**
   Ice cubes
1 **container (8 ounces) BREYERS Vanilla Lowfat Yogurt**
½ **teaspoon vanilla (optional)**
5 **tablespoons thawed COOL WHIP FREE or COOL WHIP LITE Whipped Topping**

STIR boiling water into gelatin in large bowl at least 2 minutes until completely dissolved.

MIX cold water and ice cubes to make 1 cup. Add to gelatin, stirring until slightly thickened. Remove any remaining ice. Stir in yogurt and vanilla. Pour into dessert dishes.

REFRIGERATE 1½ hours or until firm. Top with whipped topping.   *Makes 5 servings*

Nutrition Information Per Serving (using JELL-O Brand Sugar Free Low Calorie Gelatin Dessert, water and COOL WHIP FREE): 60 calories, 1g fat, less than 5mg cholesterol, 90mg sodium, 9g carbohydrate, 0g dietary fiber, 8g sugars, 3g protein

Preparation Time: 10 minutes
Refrigerating Time: 1½ hours

Yogurt Fluff

Fresh Fruit Parfaits

Whip up these fat free layered parfaits tonight!

Experiment with gelatin-fruit combinations such as orange flavor gelatin with fresh peaches; lime flavor with melon balls; or strawberry flavor with strawberries, bananas and/or blueberries.

1 cup fresh fruit
¾ cup boiling water
1 package (4-serving size) JELL-O Brand Sugar Free Low Calorie Gelatin Dessert or JELL-O Brand Gelatin Dessert, any flavor
½ cup cold water
Ice cubes
¾ cup thawed COOL WHIP FREE or COOL WHIP LITE Whipped Topping

DIVIDE fruit among 6 parfait glasses.

STIR boiling water into gelatin in medium bowl at least 2 minutes until completely dissolved. Mix cold water and ice cubes to make 1¼ cups. Add to gelatin, stirring until slightly thickened. Remove any remaining ice. Measure ¾ cup of the gelatin; pour into parfait glasses. Refrigerate 1 hour or until set but not firm (gelatin should stick to finger when touched and should mound).

STIR whipped topping into remaining gelatin with wire whisk until smooth. Spoon over gelatin in glasses.

REFRIGERATE 1 hour or until firm. Garnish as desired.   *Makes 6 servings*

Nutrition Information Per Serving (using ½ cup each blueberries and strawberries, JELL-O Brand Sugar Free Low Calorie Gelatin Dessert and COOL WHIP FREE and omitting cookies): 35 calories, 0.5g fat, 0mg cholesterol, 55mg sodium, 6g carbohydrate, less than 1g dietary fiber, 3g sugars, 1g protein, 15% daily value vitamin C

Preparation Time: 20 minutes
Refrigerating Time: 2 hours

Pudding in a Cloud

How to please the family in just 15 minutes.

2 cups thawed COOL WHIP Whipped Topping
2 cups cold milk
1 package (4-serving size) JELL-O Instant
    Pudding & Pie Filling, any flavor

Amuse the kids by letting them make faces on the pudding with pieces of marshmallow, gumdrops or decorating gel.

SPOON whipped topping evenly into 6 dessert dishes. Using back of spoon, spread whipped topping onto bottom and up side of each dish.

POUR milk into medium bowl. Add pudding mix. Beat with wire whisk 2 minutes. Let stand 5 minutes. Spoon pudding into center of whipped topping.

REFRIGERATE until ready to serve.

Makes 6 servings

Preparation Time: 15 minutes
Refrigerating Time: 2 hours

JELL-O®
Fun Facts

In the early 1920's, Angus McDonall created a series of JELL-O illustrations under the banner of "America's Most Famous Dessert At Home Everywhere." These depictions showed JELL-O served by a monk in mission country, eyed by a bear in the mountains, placed on a prairie lunch table, eaten on a doorstop in New England, washed up on a desert island, and carried into an igloo under northern lights.

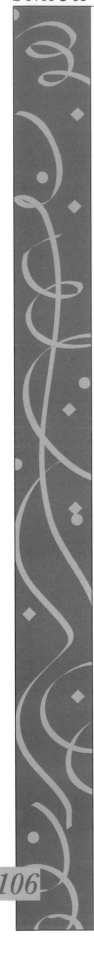

Dirt Cups

Great kid appeal here!

This recipe was developed in 1989 as part of the JELL-O Snacktivities® campaign to encourage parents and kids to make fun recipes together.

1 package (16 ounces) chocolate sandwich cookies
2 cups cold milk
1 package (4-serving size) JELL-O Chocolate Flavor Instant Pudding & Pie Filling
1 tub (8 ounces) COOL WHIP Whipped Topping, thawed
8 to 10 (7-ounce) paper or plastic cups
Suggested garnishes: gummy worms or other gummy candies, candy flowers, chopped peanuts, granola

CRUSH cookies in zipper-style plastic bag with rolling pin or in food processor.

POUR milk into large bowl. Add pudding mix. Beat with wire whisk 2 minutes. Stir in whipped topping and ½ of the crushed cookies.

PLACE about 1 tablespoon of the crushed cookies in each cup. Fill cups about ¾ full with pudding mixture. Top with remaining crushed cookies.

REFRIGERATE until ready to serve. Garnish as desired. *Makes 8 to 10 servings*

Sand Cups: Use 1 package (12 ounces) vanilla wafer cookies and JELL-O Vanilla Flavor Instant Pudding & Pie Filling.

Preparation Time: 15 minutes
Refrigerating Time: 2 hours

Left to right: Sand Cups, Dirt Cups

All-Time Favorites

Under-the-Sea Salad

Delightfully tangy with a hint of cinnamon.

- 1 can (16 ounces) pear halves in syrup, undrained
- 1 cup boiling water
- 1 package (4-serving size) JELL-O Brand Lime Flavor Gelatin Dessert
- ¼ teaspoon salt (optional)
- 1 tablespoon lemon juice
- 2 packages (3 ounces each) PHILADELPHIA BRAND Cream Cheese, softened
- ⅛ teaspoon ground cinnamon (optional)

DRAIN pears, reserving ¾ cup of the syrup. Dice pears; set aside.

STIR boiling water into gelatin and salt in medium bowl at least 2 minutes until completely dissolved. Stir in reserved syrup and lemon juice. Pour 1¼ cups gelatin into 4-cup mold or 8×4-inch loaf pan. Refrigerate about 1 hour or until set but not firm (gelatin should stick to finger when touched and should mound).

MEANWHILE, stir remaining gelatin gradually into cream cheese in large bowl with wire whisk until smooth. Stir in pears and cinnamon. Spoon over gelatin layer in mold.

REFRIGERATE 4 hours or until firm. Unmold. Garnish as desired.

Makes 6 servings

Preparation Time: 20 minutes
Refrigerating Time: 5 hours

Top to bottom: Vanilla Rice Pudding (page 113), Chocolate Swirl Cheesecake (page 116), Under-the-Sea Salad, Ribbon Squares (page 112)

Crown Jewel Dessert

The concept of creamy gelatin with clear cubes originated in 1955 with a recipe called Broken Window Glass Cake.

Shimmering gems of JELL-O make this mold extra special.

1 package (4-serving size) JELL-O Brand Lime Flavor Gelatin Dessert*
1 package (4-serving size) JELL-O Brand Orange Flavor Gelatin Dessert*
1 package (4-serving size) JELL-O Brand Strawberry Flavor Gelatin Dessert*
3 cups boiling water
1½ cups cold water
1 cup boiling water
1 package (4-serving size) JELL-O Brand Strawberry Flavor Gelatin Dessert
½ cup cold water
1 tub (8 ounces) COOL WHIP Whipped Topping, thawed

PREPARE lime, orange and 1 package strawberry gelatin separately as directed on packages, using 1 cup boiling water and ½ cup cold water for each. Pour each flavor into separate 8-inch square pans. Refrigerate 4 hours or until firm. Cut into ½-inch cubes; measure 1½ cups of each flavor. (Use the remaining gelatin cubes for garnish if desired or for snacking.)

STIR 1 cup boiling water into remaining package of strawberry gelatin in medium bowl at least 2 minutes until completely dissolved. Stir in ½ cup cold water. Refrigerate 45 minutes or until slightly thickened (consistency of unbeaten egg whites).

STIR in ½ of the whipped topping. Gently stir in measured gelatin cubes. Pour into 9×5-inch loaf pan.

REFRIGERATE 4 hours or until firm. Unmold. Garnish with remaining whipped topping and gelatin cubes, if desired.   *Makes 16 servings*

*Or use any 3 different flavors of JELL-O Brand Gelatin Dessert.

Preparation Time: 45 minutes
Refrigerating Time: 8¾ hours

Crown Jewel Dessert

Ribbon Squares

3 cups boiling water
1 package (4-serving size) JELL-O Brand Gelatin Dessert, any red flavor
1 package (4-serving size) JELL-O Brand Lemon Flavor Gelatin Dessert
1 package (4-serving size) JELL-O Brand Lime Flavor Gelatin Dessert
1½ cups cold water
1 package (8 ounces) PHILADELPHIA BRAND Cream Cheese, softened
1 can (8 ounces) crushed pineapple in juice, undrained
1 cup thawed COOL WHIP Whipped Topping
½ cup KRAFT Mayo: Real Mayonnaise

Canned pineapple works perfectly in gelatin salads and desserts. Fresh pineapple, however, contains an enzyme that prevents gelatin from setting so it should never be used as an ingredient when preparing JELL-O.

STIR 1 cup boiling water into each flavor of gelatin in separate medium bowls at least 2 minutes until completely dissolved. Stir ¾ cup of the cold water into red gelatin. Pour into 9-inch square pan. Refrigerate about 45 minutes or until set but not firm (gelatin should stick to finger when touched and should mound).

MEANWHILE, stir lemon gelatin gradually into cream cheese in large bowl with wire whisk until smooth. Stir in pineapple with juice. Refrigerate about 45 minutes or until slightly thickened (consistency of unbeaten egg whites). Stir in whipped topping and mayonnaise. Spoon over red gelatin layer in pan. Refrigerate about 30 minutes or until set but not firm (gelatin should stick to finger when touched and should mound).

MEANWHILE, stir remaining ¾ cup cold water into lime gelatin. Refrigerate about 30 minutes or until slightly thickened (consistency of unbeaten egg whites). Spoon over lemon gelatin mixture in pan.

REFRIGERATE 4 hours or until firm. Unmold. Cut into squares. Garnish as desired.

Makes 9 servings

Preparation Time: 30 minutes
Refrigerating Time: 5¼ hours

Vanilla Rice Pudding

Comfort food at its best—quick and easy, too.

- 1 package (4-serving size) JELL-O Vanilla or Coconut Cream Flavor Cook & Serve Pudding & Pie Filling (*not Instant*)
- 4 cups milk
- 1 egg, well beaten
- 1 cup MINUTE Original Instant Enriched Rice, uncooked
- ¼ cup raisins (optional)
- ¼ teaspoon ground cinnamon*
- ⅛ teaspoon ground nutmeg*

Created in 1959 for a MINUTE Rice advertisement, Vanilla Rice Pudding combined two early convenience products to make a favorite traditional family dessert.

STIR pudding mix into milk and egg in large saucepan. Stir in rice and raisins.

STIRRING constantly, cook on medium heat until mixture comes to full boil. Remove from heat. Cool 5 minutes, stirring twice.

POUR into dessert dishes or serving bowl. Serve warm or refrigerate until ready to serve. (For chilled pudding, place plastic wrap on surface of hot pudding. Refrigerate about 1 hour. Stir before serving.) Sprinkle with cinnamon and nutmeg. Garnish as desired. *Makes 8 servings*

*Cinnamon and nutmeg can be added before cooking but pudding will be darker.

Note: *Recipe can be doubled.*

Preparation Time: 5 minutes
Cooking Time: 25 minutes

Striped Delight

This perennial favorite, combining cream cheese, whipped topping and instant pudding, was first made in 1983 and was originally called Cream Cheese Pudding Dessert.

A potluck favorite, this creamy dessert features a chocolatey pudding layer over a pecan shortbread crust.

1 cup flour
1 cup finely chopped pecans
¼ cup sugar (optional)
½ cup (1 stick) butter or margarine, melted
1 package (8 ounces) PHILADELPHIA BRAND Cream Cheese, softened
¼ cup sugar
2 tablespoons milk
1 tub (8 ounces) COOL WHIP Whipped Topping, thawed
3½ cups cold milk
2 packages (4-serving size) JELL-O Chocolate Flavor Instant Pudding & Pie Filling

HEAT oven to 350°F.

MIX flour, pecans and ¼ cup sugar in 13×9-inch baking pan. Stir in butter until flour is moistened. Press firmly onto bottom of pan. Bake 20 minutes or until lightly browned. Cool.

BEAT cream cheese, ¼ cup sugar and 2 tablespoons milk in large bowl with wire whisk until smooth. Gently stir in ½ of the whipped topping. Spread onto cooled crust.

POUR 3½ cups milk into large bowl. Add pudding mixes. Beat with wire whisk 1 to 2 minutes or until well blended. Pour over cream cheese layer.

REFRIGERATE 4 hours or until set. Just before serving, spread remaining whipped topping over pudding. Garnish as desired.

Makes 15 servings

Preparation Time: 30 minutes
Baking Time: 20 minutes
Refrigerating Time: 4 hours

Striped Delight

Chocolate Swirl Cheesecake

Create this elegant showpiece dessert in just minutes.

1 package (11.1 ounces) JELL-O No Bake Real Cheesecake
2 tablespoons sugar
⅓ cup butter or margarine, melted
2 squares BAKER'S Semi-Sweet Baking Chocolate
1½ cups cold milk, divided

MIX crumbs, sugar and butter thoroughly with fork in 9-inch pie plate until crumbs are well moistened. Press firmly against side of pie plate first, using finger or large spoon to shape edge. Press remaining crumbs firmly onto bottom of pie plate using measuring cup.

MICROWAVE chocolate and 2 tablespoons of the milk in microwavable bowl on HIGH 1½ minutes or until chocolate is almost melted. Stir until chocolate is completely melted.

BEAT remaining milk and filling mix with electric mixer on low speed until blended. Beat on medium speed 3 minutes. (Filling will be thick.) Spoon 2 cups of the filling into crust. Stir chocolate mixture into remaining filling. Spoon over cheesecake. Swirl with knife to marbleize.

REFRIGERATE at least 1 hour.

Makes 8 servings

Preparation Time: 15 minutes
Refrigerating Time: 1 hour

"Never Do to be Without Jell-O."

As Tommy finished the Jell-O® dessert at dinner mamma remarked, "That's the last of the Jell-O® in the house," and he proceeded to the kitchen to enter an order for more.

"Never do to be without Jell-O," Tommy says.

Good idea, too, for with

JELL-O®

in the house you have something to rely on in time of emergency and all other times.

Any woman can make a dozen or more different kinds of dishes from each of the six flavors of Jell-O® which are: Strawberry, Raspberry, Orange, Lemon, Cherry, Chocolate.

Send for the 1920 Jell-O Book, which contains some new recipes for popular dishes.

THE GENESEE PURE FOOD COMPANY
Le Roy, N. Y., and Bridgeburg, Ont.

1921

Better-Than-S_x Cake

Try it . . . you'll like it!

1½ cups graham cracker crumbs

⅔ cup chopped pecans, divided

½ cup (1 stick) butter or margarine, melted

6 tablespoons sugar

1 package (8 ounces) PHILADELPHIA BRAND Cream Cheese, softened

3½ cups cold milk

2 packages (4-serving size) JELL-O Vanilla Flavor Instant Pudding & Pie Filling

1⅓ cups BAKER'S ANGEL FLAKE Coconut, divided

1 tub (8 ounces) COOL WHIP Whipped Topping, thawed

This rich layered pudding dessert, created in 1980 as Layered Coconut Pecan Delight, just shows how times change but good taste doesn't!

MIX crumbs, ⅓ cup of the pecans, butter and sugar in 13×9-inch pan. Press firmly onto bottom of pan.

BEAT cream cheese in large bowl with electric mixer on low speed until smooth. Gradually beat in ½ cup of the milk. Add remaining milk and the pudding mixes. Beat on low speed about 2 minutes or until well blended. Stir in 1 cup of the coconut. Pour immediately over crust. Spread whipped topping evenly over the pudding mixture.

REFRIGERATE 2 hours or until set. Toast remaining ⅓ cup coconut and ⅓ cup pecans. Sprinkle over top of dessert.   *Makes 15 servings*

Preparation Time: 30 minutes
Refrigerating Time: 2 hours

117

Rainbow Ribbon Mold

A real showpiece for a buffet or dinner party.

Gelatin recipes with layers of different flavors and textures date back to the early 1900's when they were called Neapolitans. They were often molded in loaf pans and served in slices to show the rainbow effect.

6¼ cups boiling water
5 packages (4-serving size) JELL-O Brand
   Gelatin Dessert, any 5 different flavors
1 cup (½ pint) BREAKSTONE'S Sour Cream
   or BREYERS Vanilla Lowfat Yogurt

STIR 1¼ cups boiling water into 1 flavor of gelatin in small bowl at least 2 minutes until completely dissolved. Pour ¾ cup of the dissolved gelatin into 6-cup ring mold. Refrigerate about 15 minutes until set but not firm (gelatin should stick to finger when touched and should mound). Refrigerate remaining gelatin in bowl about 5 minutes until slightly thickened (consistency of unbeaten egg whites). Gradually stir in 3 tablespoons of the sour cream. Spoon over gelatin in pan. Refrigerate about 15 minutes or until set but not firm (gelatin should stick to finger when touched and should mound).

MEANWHILE, repeat process with each remaining gelatin flavor. (Be sure to cool dissolved gelatin to room temperature before pouring into mold.) Refrigerate gelatin as directed to create a total of 10 alternating clear and creamy gelatin layers.

REFRIGERATE 2 hours or until firm. Unmold. Garnish as desired.   *Makes 12 servings*

Preparation Time: 1 hour
Refrigerating Time: 4½ hours

JELL-O®
Fun Facts

JELL-O gelatin is the largest-selling prepared dessert in America.

Rainbow Ribbon Mold

Creamy Vanilla Sauce

Developed in 1981 for a JELL-O Instant Pudding advertisement, variations on this sauce made with other pudding flavors have topped many a dessert.

An elegant topping for fresh fruit or gingerbread.

**3½ cups cold milk, light cream or half-and-half
1 package (4-serving size) JELL-O Vanilla or French Vanilla Flavor Instant Pudding & Pie Filling**

POUR milk into bowl. Add pudding mix. Beat with wire whisk 2 minutes. Cover.

REFRIGERATE until ready to serve. Serve over your favorite fruits or cake. Garnish as desired.

Makes 3½ cups

Creamy Citrus Sauce: Add 2 teaspoons grated orange peel with pudding mix.

Preparation Time: 5 minutes

Mini Chocolate Tarts

Chocolate Silk Pie, the second JELL-O No Bake Dessert, joined the line in 1984.

Enjoy a touch of elegance with these silky smooth miniature desserts.

**1 package (9.2 ounces) JELL-O No Bake Chocolate Silk Pie
⅓ cup butter or margarine, melted
1⅔ cups cold milk**

MIX crumbs and butter thoroughly with fork in small bowl until crumbs are well moistened. Press onto bottoms of 12 paper-lined muffin cups.

BEAT milk and filling mix with electric mixer on low speed until blended. Beat on medium speed 3 minutes. (Filling will be thick.) Spoon over crumb mixture in muffin cups.

REFRIGERATE at least 1 hour or until ready to serve.

Makes 12

Preparation Time: 15 minutes
Refrigerating Time: 1 hour

Dream Pie

This heavenly pie lives up to its name.

> 2 envelopes DREAM WHIP Whipped Topping Mix
> 2¾ cups cold milk, divided
> 1 teaspoon vanilla
> 2 packages (4-serving size) JELL-O Instant Pudding & Pie Filling, any flavor
> 1 baked pastry shell (9 inch), cooled, or
>   1 prepared graham cracker or chocolate flavor crumb crust (6 ounces)

BEAT whipped topping mix, 1 cup of the milk and vanilla in large bowl with electric mixer on high speed 6 minutes or until topping thickens and forms peaks.

ADD remaining 1¾ cups milk and pudding mixes; beat on low speed until blended. Beat on high speed 2 minutes, scraping bowl occasionally. Spoon into pastry shell.

REFRIGERATE at least 4 hours.

Makes 8 servings

Preparation Time: 15 minutes
Refrigerating Time: 4 hours

During World War II, one-crust pies became popular because of the scarcity of shortening. Many were filled with JELL-O gelatin or pudding—convenient products for women involved in the war effort.

JELL-O Fun Facts

In 1913, Rosie O'Neill, creator of the famous rosy-cheeked Kewpie Dolls, illustrated a full-color Kewpie Doll JELL-O Book, showing the little imps making and garnishing a variety of beautiful salads and desserts.

Luscious Pies

Strawberry Lime Pie

This fluffy concoction beautifully complements the tartness of fresh berries.

⅔ cup boiling water
1 package (4-serving size) JELL-O Brand Lime Flavor Gelatin Dessert
½ teaspoon grated lime peel
2 tablespoons lime juice
½ cup cold water
Ice cubes
1 tub (8 ounces) COOL WHIP Whipped Topping, thawed
1 cup sliced strawberries
1 prepared graham cracker crumb crust (6 ounces)

STIR boiling water into gelatin in large bowl at least 2 minutes until completely dissolved. Stir in lime peel and juice. Mix cold water and ice to make 1 cup. Add to gelatin, stirring until slightly thickened. Remove any remaining ice.

STIR in 2½ cups of the whipped topping with wire whisk until smooth. Gently stir in strawberries. Refrigerate 30 minutes or until mixture is very thick and will mound. Spoon into crust.

REFRIGERATE 4 hours or until firm. Top with remaining whipped topping. Garnish as desired. *Makes 8 servings*

Preparation Time: 20 minutes
Refrigerating Time: 4½ hours

123

Top to bottom: Glazed Fruit Pie (page 126), Cookies-and-Cream Pie (page 127), Strawberry Lime Pie, White Chocolate-Devil's Food Pie (page 134)

Chocolate Mallow Cookie Pie

This will be a big hit with the family!

An American family favorite for nearly 70 years, JELL-O Pudding & Instant Pie Filling is now available in 51 flavor varieties.

2 cups miniature marshmallows
2 tablespoons milk
2½ cups thawed COOL WHIP Whipped Topping
2 cups cold milk
2 packages (4-serving size) JELL-O Chocolate Flavor Instant Pudding & Pie Filling
1 prepared chocolate flavor crumb crust (6 ounces)
14 vanilla wafers
Chocolate Topping (recipe follows, optional)

MICROWAVE marshmallows and 2 tablespoons milk in medium microwavable bowl on HIGH 1 minute, stirring after 30 seconds. Stir until marshmallows are melted. Refrigerate 15 minutes to cool. Gently stir in 1 cup of the whipped topping.

POUR 2 cups milk into large bowl. Add pudding mixes. Beat with wire whisk just until mixed. Immediately stir in remaining whipped topping.

SPOON pudding mixture into crust. Arrange cookies on top. Spread marshmallow mixture over cookies. Drizzle with Chocolate Topping, if desired.

REFRIGERATE 4 hours or until set.

Makes 8 servings

Chocolate Topping: Microwave 2 squares BAKER'S Semi-Sweet Baking Chocolate in heavy zipper-style plastic sandwich bag on HIGH 1 to 2 minutes or until chocolate is almost melted. Add 2 teaspoons softened butter; gently squeeze bag until chocolate and butter are completely melted. Fold down top of bag; snip tiny piece off 1 corner from bottom of bag to drizzle chocolate.

Preparation Time: 30 minutes
Refrigerating Time: 4¼ hours

Chocolate Mallow Cookie Pie

Glazed Fruit Pie

This creamy pie, topped with fruit encased in clear gelatin, was first featured in a 1985 television commercial for JELL-O brand pudding.

Try different fruits and JELL-O pudding flavors to create variations of this fabulous pie.

- **1½ cups cold milk or half-and-half**
- **1 package (4-serving size) JELL-O Vanilla Flavor Instant Pudding & Pie Filling**
- **1 prepared graham cracker crumb crust (6 ounces) or 1 baked pastry shell (9 inch), cooled**
- **1 cup boiling water**
- **1 package (4-serving size) JELL-O Brand Lemon, Peach or Orange Flavor Gelatin Dessert, or any red flavor**
- **½ cup cold water**
- **1½ cups fresh or drained canned fruit***

POUR milk into large bowl. Add pudding mix. Beat with wire whisk 1 minute. Pour into crust. Refrigerate 1 hour.

STIR boiling water into gelatin in large bowl at least 2 minutes until completely dissolved. Stir in cold water. Refrigerate 1 hour or until thickened (spoon drawn through leaves definite impression). Pour 1 cup gelatin over the pudding layer. Arrange fruit on gelatin. Spoon remaining gelatin over fruit.

REFRIGERATE 2 hours or until firm.

Makes 8 servings

*Use any variety of berries, mandarin orange sections, sliced bananas, peaches or plums, or halved seedless grapes.

Preparation Time: 15 minutes
Refrigerating Time: 4 hours

Ice Cream Shop Pie

Favorite ice cream flavors in a quick-to-make pie.

1½ cups cold milk, half-and-half or light cream
1 package (4-serving size) JELL-O Instant Pudding & Pie Filling
1 tub (8 ounces) COOL WHIP Whipped Topping, thawed
1 prepared crumb crust (6 ounces)

POUR milk into large bowl. Add pudding mix. Beat with wire whisk 2 minutes. Gently stir in whipped topping. Spoon into crust.

FREEZE 6 hours or overnight until firm. Let stand at room temperature or in refrigerator 15 minutes or until pie can be cut easily.

GARNISH as desired.   *Makes 8 servings*

Cookies-and-Cream Pie: Use JELL-O Vanilla Flavor Instant Pudding & Pie Filling and chocolate crumb crust. Stir in 1 cup chopped chocolate sandwich cookies with whipped topping.

Rocky Road Pie: Use JELL-O Chocolate Flavor Instant Pudding & Pie Filling and chocolate crumb crust. Stir in ⅓ cup each BAKER'S Semi-Sweet Real Chocolate Chips, miniature marshmallows and chopped nuts with whipped topping. Serve with chocolate sauce, if desired.

Peanut Butter Pie: Use JELL-O Vanilla Flavor Instant Pudding & Pie Filling and graham cracker crumb crust. Reduce milk to 1 cup and add ½ cup peanut butter with pudding mix. Serve with chocolate sauce and chopped peanuts, if desired.

Preparation Time: 15 minutes
Freezing Time: 6 hours

Instant pudding & pie filling and whipped topping provide the base for these delectable freezer pies with a variety of stir-in ingredients.

127

Lemon Chiffon Pie

Cool, easy and incredibly delicious!

⅔ **cup boiling water**
1 **package (4-serving size) JELL-O Brand Lemon Flavor Gelatin Dessert**
2 **teaspoons grated lemon peel**
2 **tablespoons lemon juice**
½ **cup cold water**
   Ice cubes
1 **tub (8 ounces) COOL WHIP Whipped Topping, thawed**
1 **prepared graham cracker crumb crust (6 ounces)**

STIR boiling water into gelatin in large bowl at least 2 minutes until completely dissolved. Stir in lemon peel and juice. Mix cold water and ice to make 1¼ cups. Add to gelatin, stirring until slightly thickened. Remove any remaining ice.

STIR in whipped topping with wire whisk until smooth. Refrigerate 20 to 30 minutes or until mixture is very thick and will mound. Spoon into crust.

REFRIGERATE 6 hours or overnight until firm. Garnish as desired.　　*Makes 8 servings*

Preparation Time: 20 minutes
Refrigerating Time: 6½ hours

Carly Simon eats JELL-O before every performance to soothe her nerves.

Lemon Chiffon Pie

Double Layer Chocolate Pie

To quickly soften cream cheese, microwave on HIGH for 15 to 20 seconds.

4 ounces PHILADELPHIA BRAND Cream Cheese, softened
1 tablespoon milk or half-and-half
1 tablespoon sugar
1 tub (8 ounces) COOL WHIP Whipped Topping, thawed
1 prepared chocolate flavor crumb crust (6 ounces)
2 cups cold milk or half-and-half
2 packages (4-serving size) JELL-O Chocolate Flavor Instant Pudding & Pie Filling

MIX cream cheese, 1 tablespoon milk and sugar in large bowl with wire whisk until smooth. Gently stir in 1½ cups of the whipped topping. Spread onto bottom of crust.

POUR 2 cups milk into bowl. Add pudding mixes. Beat with wire whisk until well mixed. (Mixture will be thick.) Immediately stir in remaining whipped topping. Spread over cream cheese layer.

REFRIGERATE 4 hours or until set. Garnish as desired.   *Makes 8 servings*

Preparation Time: 15 minutes
Refrigerating Time: 4 hours

JELL-O® Fun Facts

In addition to Bill Cosby, famous spokespeople for JELL-O have included Jack Benny, Andy Griffith and Ethel Barrymore.

Double Layer Chocolate Pie

Summer Berry Pie

Pure joy is this fresh berry pie!

Strawberry is, hands down, the most popular flavor of JELL-O and has been for 100 years.

¾ **cup sugar**
3 **tablespoons cornstarch**
1½ **cups water**
1 **package (4-serving size) JELL-O Brand Gelatin Dessert, any red flavor**
1 **cup blueberries**
1 **cup raspberries**
1 **cup sliced strawberries**
1 **prepared graham cracker crumb crust (6 ounces)**
2 **cups thawed COOL WHIP Whipped Topping**

MIX sugar and cornstarch in medium saucepan. Gradually stir in water until smooth. Stirring constantly, cook on medium heat until mixture comes to boil; boil 1 minute. Remove from heat. Stir in gelatin until completely dissolved. Cool to room temperature. Stir in berries. Pour into crust.

REFRIGERATE 3 hours or until firm. Top with whipped topping.   *Makes 8 servings*

Preparation Time: 20 minutes
Refrigerating Time: 3 hours

JELL-O® *Fun Facts*

Every day more than 820,000 packages of JELL-O are purchased or prepared and eaten.

Summer Berry Pie

White Chocolate-Devil's Food Pie

JELL-O Fat Free Instant Pudding & Pie Filling, specially formulated to work with skim milk, was introduced in 1994 for those seeking ways to reduce fat in their diets.

Creamy dark and white chocolate pudding layers team together to make a scrumptious dessert.

2 cups cold skim milk, divided
1 package (4-serving size) JELL-O Devil's Food Flavor Fat Free Instant Pudding & Pie Filling
1 tub (8 ounces) COOL WHIP FREE or COOL WHIP LITE Whipped Topping, thawed
1 prepared reduced fat graham cracker crumb crust (6 ounces)
1 package (4-serving size) JELL-O White Chocolate Flavor Fat Free Instant Pudding & Pie Filling

POUR 1 cup of the milk into medium bowl. Add devil's food flavor pudding mix. Beat with wire whisk 1 minute. (Mixture will be thick.) Gently stir in ½ of the whipped topping. Spoon evenly into crust.

POUR remaining 1 cup milk into another medium bowl. Add white chocolate flavor pudding mix. Beat with wire whisk 1 minute. (Mixture will be thick.) Gently stir in remaining whipped topping. Spread over pudding layer in crust.

REFRIGERATE 4 hours or until set. Garnish as desired. *Makes 8 servings*

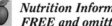 *Nutrition Information Per Serving (using COOL WHIP FREE and omitting garnish):* 270 calories, 5g fat, 0mg cholesterol, 490mg sodium, 53g carbohydrate, less than 1g dietary fiber, 4g protein, 10% daily value calcium

Preparation Time: 10 minutes
Refrigerating Time: 4 hours

Creamy Chocolate Pie

This will delight family and guests alike.

1¾ cups cold milk
2 packages (4-serving size) JELL-O Chocolate
    or Chocolate Fudge Flavor Instant
    Pudding & Pie Filling
1 tub (8 ounces) COOL WHIP Whipped
    Topping, thawed
1 prepared chocolate flavor crumb crust
    (6 ounces)

Preparation time for this luscious pie takes only 10 minutes.

POUR milk into large bowl. Add pudding mixes. Beat with wire whisk until well mixed. (Mixture will be thick.) Immediately stir in whipped topping. Spoon into crust.

REFRIGERATE 4 hours or until set. Garnish as desired. *Makes 8 servings*

Preparation Time: 10 minutes
Refrigerating Time: 4 hours

JELL-O Fun Facts

A JELL-O cartoon ad contest in 1921 challenged people to write or design a JELL-O ad. The $200 first prize was awarded based on "intelligence, composition, neatness, originality and availability." The winning ad and a photo of the creator were published four months later. The prize money was used to buy a horse.

135

Sensational Desserts

Pudding Poke Cake

A favorite with everyone . . . and so easy to make.

> 1 package (2-layer size) chocolate cake mix or cake mix with
>   pudding in the mix
> 4 cups cold milk
> 2 packages (4-serving size) JELL-O Vanilla Flavor Instant
>   Pudding & Pie Filling

PREPARE and bake cake mix as directed on package for 13×9-inch baking pan. Remove from oven. Immediately poke holes down through cake to pan at 1-inch intervals with round handle of a wooden spoon. (Or poke holes with a plastic drinking straw, using turning motion to make large holes.)

POUR milk into large bowl. Add pudding mixes. Beat with wire whisk 2 minutes. Quickly pour about ½ of the thin pudding mixture evenly over warm cake and into holes. Let remaining pudding mixture stand to thicken slightly. Spoon over top of cake, swirling to frost cake.

REFRIGERATE at least 1 hour or until ready to serve.

Makes 15 servings

Preparation Time: 30 minutes
Baking Time: 40 minutes
Refrigerating Time: 1 hour

Top to bottom: Strawberry Lime Dessert (page 141), Orange Pineapple Layered Dessert (page 140), Layered Chocolate Cheesecake Squares (page 145), Pudding Poke Cake

Lemon Soufflé Cheesecake

A stunning dessert your guests will adore.

JELL-O gelatin is the largest-selling prepared dessert in America.

1 graham cracker, crushed, or 2 tablespoons graham cracker crumbs, divided
⅔ cup boiling water
1 package (4-serving size) JELL-O Brand Lemon Flavor Sugar Free Low Calorie Gelatin Dessert or JELL-O Brand Lemon Flavor Gelatin Dessert
1 cup LIGHT N' LIVELY 1% Lowfat Cottage Cheese with Calcium
1 tub (8 ounces) PHILADELPHIA BRAND LIGHT Light Cream Cheese
2 cups thawed COOL WHIP FREE or COOL WHIP LITE Whipped Topping

SPRINKLE ½ of the crumbs onto side of 8- or 9-inch springform pan or 9-inch pie plate that has been sprayed with no stick cooking spray.

STIR boiling water into gelatin in large bowl at least 2 minutes until completely dissolved. Pour into blender container. Add cheeses; cover. Blend on medium speed until smooth, scraping down sides occasionally.

POUR into large bowl. Gently stir in whipped topping. Pour into prepared pan; smooth top. Sprinkle remaining crumbs around outside edge. Refrigerate 4 hours or until set.

REMOVE side of pan just before serving. Garnish as desired. *Makes 8 servings*

Nutrition Information Per Serving (using JELL-O Brand Lemon Flavor Sugar Free Low Calorie Gelatin Dessert and COOL WHIP FREE and omitting garnish): *130 calories, 6g fat, 20mg cholesterol, 280mg sodium, 11g carbohydrate, 0g dietary fiber, 5g sugars, 7g protein, 10% daily value calcium*

Preparation Time: 20 minutes
Refrigerating Time: 4 hours

Lemon Soufflé Cheesecake

Orange Pineapple Layered Dessert

Some fruits sink and others float when added to JELL-O. Sinkers include mandarin oranges, seedless grapes and drained slices or chunks of canned fruits. Floaters are slices of banana, apple, strawberries, fresh peaches and pears, and fresh orange sections.

Even the kids will love this tasty dessert perfect for family gatherings.

1½ **cups boiling water**
1 **package (8-serving size) or 2 packages (4-serving size) JELL-O Brand Orange Flavor Gelatin Dessert**
1 **cup cold water**
1 **can (20 ounces) crushed pineapple in juice, undrained**
1 **can (11 ounces) mandarin orange segments, drained**
1½ **cups graham cracker crumbs**
½ **cup sugar, divided**
½ **cup (1 stick) butter or margarine, melted**
1 **package (8 ounces) PHILADELPHIA BRAND Cream Cheese, softened**
2 **tablespoons milk**
1 **tub (8 ounces) COOL WHIP Whipped Topping, thawed**

STIR boiling water into gelatin in large bowl at least 2 minutes until completely dissolved. Stir in cold water, pineapple with juice and oranges. Refrigerate about 1¼ hours or until slightly thickened (consistency of unbeaten egg whites).

MIX crumbs, ¼ cup of the sugar and butter in 13×9-inch pan. Press firmly onto bottom of pan. Refrigerate until ready to fill.

BEAT cream cheese, remaining ¼ cup sugar and milk in large bowl until smooth. Gently stir in 2 cups of the whipped topping. Spread evenly over crust. Spoon gelatin over cream cheese layer.

REFRIGERATE 3 hours or until firm. Garnish with remaining whipped topping.   *Makes 15 servings*

Preparation Time: 30 minutes
Refrigerating Time: 4¼ hours

Strawberry Lime Dessert

2 cups boiling water
1 package (4-serving size) JELL-O Brand Lime Flavor Sugar Free Low Calorie Gelatin Dessert or JELL-O Brand Lime Flavor Gelatin Dessert
½ cup cold water
1 container (8 ounces) BREYERS Vanilla Lowfat Yogurt
1 package (4-serving size) JELL-O Brand Strawberry Flavor Sugar Free Low Calorie Gelatin Dessert or JELL-O Brand Strawberry Flavor Gelatin Dessert
1 package (10 ounces) frozen strawberries in lite syrup, unthawed

Fruits frequently used in early recipes were strawberries, peaches, pineapple, apricots, cherries, prunes, raisins, dates and bananas.

STIR 1 cup of the boiling water into lime gelatin in medium bowl at least 2 minutes until completely dissolved. Stir in cold water. Refrigerate about 45 minutes or until slightly thickened (consistency of unbeaten egg whites). Stir in yogurt with wire whisk until smooth. Pour into 2-quart serving bowl. Refrigerate about 15 minutes or until set but not firm (gelatin should stick to finger when touched and should mound).

STIR remaining 1 cup boiling water into strawberry gelatin in medium bowl at least 2 minutes until completely dissolved. Stir in frozen berries until berries are separated and gelatin is thickened (spoon drawn through leaves definite impression). Spoon over lime gelatin mixture.

REFRIGERATE 2 hours or until firm. Garnish as desired. *Makes 10 servings*

Nutrition Information Per Serving (using JELL-O Brand Strawberry and Lime Flavors Sugar Free Low Calorie Gelatin Dessert and omitting garnish): 60 calories, 0g fat, less than 5mg cholesterol, 65mg sodium, 11g carbohydrate, less than 1g dietary fiber, 9g sugars, 2g protein, 15% daily value vitamin C

Preparation Time: 15 minutes
Refrigerating Time: 3 hours

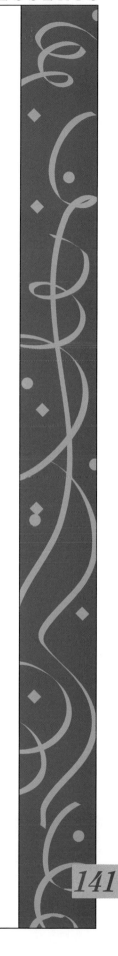

Peach Melba Dessert

Peach Melba was created in the late 1800's by renowned French chef Escoffier for Dame Nellie Melba, an Australian opera singer. The original version featured peach halves topped with vanilla ice cream, raspberry sauce, whipped cream and sliced almonds.

1½ cups boiling water
2 packages (4-serving size) JELL-O Brand Raspberry Flavor Sugar Free Low Calorie Gelatin Dessert or JELL-O Brand Raspberry Flavor Gelatin Dessert
1 container (8 ounces) BREYERS Vanilla Lowfat Yogurt
1 cup raspberries, divided
1 can (8 ounces) peach slices in juice, undrained
Cold water

STIR ¾ cup of the boiling water into 1 package of gelatin in large bowl at least 2 minutes until completely dissolved. Refrigerate about 1 hour or until slightly thickened (consistency of unbeaten egg whites). Stir in yogurt and ½ cup of the raspberries. Reserve remaining raspberries for garnish. Pour gelatin mixture into serving bowl. Refrigerate about 2 hours or until set but not firm (gelatin should stick to finger when touched and should mound).

MEANWHILE, drain peaches, reserving juice. Add cold water to reserved juice to make 1 cup; set aside. Stir remaining ¾ cup boiling water into remaining package of gelatin in large bowl at least 2 minutes until completely dissolved. Stir in measured juice and water. Refrigerate about 1 hour or until slightly thickened (consistency of unbeaten egg whites).

RESERVE several peach slices for garnish; chop remaining peaches. Stir chopped peaches into slightly thickened gelatin. Spoon over gelatin layer in bowl. Refrigerate 3 hours or until firm. Top with reserved fruits.   *Makes 8 servings*

Nutrition Information Per Serving (using JELL-O Brand Raspberry Flavor Sugar Free Low Calorie Gelatin Dessert): 60 calories, 0g fat, less than 5mg cholesterol, 75mg sodium, 10g carbohydrate, 1g dietary fiber, 11g sugars, 3g protein

Preparation Time: 20 minutes
Refrigerating Time: 6 hours

143

Peach Melba Dessert

Fruity Pound Cake

A wonderfully moist cake with just the right touch of lemon.

> 1 package (4-serving size) JELL-O Brand Lemon Flavor Gelatin Dessert
> 1 teaspoon grated lemon or orange peel
> 1 package (2-layer size) white cake mix or cake mix with pudding in the mix
> ¾ cup water
> ¼ cup oil
> 4 eggs
> Fluffy Pudding Frosting (recipe follows)

ADD gelatin and grated peel to cake mix.

PREPARE and bake cake mix as directed on package in two 8- or 9-inch round cake pans. Cool 15 minutes; remove from pans. Cool completely on wire racks. Fill and frost with Fluffy Pudding Frosting. Decorate as desired.   *Makes 12 servings*

Fluffy Pudding Frosting: Pour 1 cup cold milk into medium bowl. Add 1 package (4-serving size) JELL-O Instant Pudding & Pie Filling, any flavor, and ¼ cup powdered sugar. Beat with wire whisk 2 minutes. Gently stir in 1 tub (8 ounces) COOL WHIP Whipped Topping, thawed. Spread onto cake at once. Makes about 4 cups or enough for two 8- or 9-inch layers.

Preparation Time: 30 minutes
Baking Time: 40 minutes

Now's the time for JELL-O
SIX DELICIOUS FLAVORS

1952

Layered Chocolate Cheesecake Squares

This is the ultimate dessert for dinner guests.

1 package (9.2 ounces) JELL-O No Bake Chocolate Silk Pie
1 package (11.1 ounces) JELL-O No Bake Real Cheesecake
½ cup (1 stick) butter or margarine, melted
1⅔ cups cold milk
1½ cups cold milk

This recipe was developed in 1984 with the introduction of JELL-O No Bake Chocolate Silk Pie.

MIX crumbs from both packages and butter thoroughly with fork in medium bowl until crumbs are well moistened. Press firmly onto bottom of foil-lined 13×9-inch pan.

PREPARE Chocolate Silk Pie and Cheesecake fillings, separately, as directed on each package. Spread chocolate filling evenly over crust; top with cheesecake filling.

REFRIGERATE at least 1 hour. Garnish as desired.

Makes 15 servings

Preparation Time: 20 minutes
Refrigerating Time: 1 hour

JELL-O®
Fun Facts

In 1943, a JELL-O ad featured singer Kate Smith with a wartime message on managing scarce and rationed foods: "We can be careful to buy and cook only what we need! And we can think up smart ways to use leftovers."

ℬerried Delight

A new berry season sensation.

1½ cups graham cracker crumbs
½ cup sugar, divided
½ cup (1 stick) butter or margarine, melted
1 package (8 ounces) PHILADELPHIA BRAND Cream Cheese, softened
2 tablespoons milk
1 tub (8 ounces) COOL WHIP Whipped Topping, thawed
2 pints strawberries, hulled, halved
3½ cups cold milk
2 packages (4-serving size) JELL-O Vanilla Flavor Instant Pudding & Pie Filling

MIX crumbs, ¼ cup of the sugar and butter in 13×9-inch pan. Press firmly onto bottom of pan. Refrigerate until ready to fill.

BEAT cream cheese, remaining ¼ cup sugar and 2 tablespoons milk until smooth. Gently stir in ½ of the whipped topping. Spread over crust. Top with strawberry halves.

POUR 3½ cups milk into large bowl. Add pudding mixes. Beat with wire whisk 2 minutes. Pour over cream cheese layer.

REFRIGERATE 4 hours or until set. Just before serving, spread remaining whipped topping over pudding.   *Makes 15 servings*

Preparation Time: 30 minutes
Refrigerating Time: 4 hours

Berried Delight

Holiday Specialties

Holiday Poke Cake

This all-time favorite is appropriately red and green for the Yuletide festivities.

    2 baked 8- or 9-inch round white cake layers, cooled completely
    2 cups boiling water
    1 package (4-serving size) JELL-O Brand Gelatin Dessert, any
        red flavor
    1 package (4-serving size) JELL-O Brand Lime Flavor Gelatin
        Dessert
    1 tub (8 or 12 ounces) COOL WHIP Whipped Topping, thawed

PLACE cake layers, top sides up, in 2 clean 8- or 9-inch round cake pans. Pierce cake with large fork at ½-inch intervals.

STIR 1 cup of the boiling water into each flavor of gelatin in separate bowls at least 2 minutes until completely dissolved. Carefully pour red gelatin over 1 cake layer and lime gelatin over second cake layer. Refrigerate 3 hours.

DIP 1 cake pan in warm water 10 seconds; unmold onto serving plate. Spread with about 1 cup of the whipped topping. Unmold second cake layer; carefully place on first cake layer. Frost top and side of cake with remaining whipped topping.

REFRIGERATE at least 1 hour or until ready to serve. Decorate as desired. *Makes 12 servings*

Preparation Time: 30 minutes
Refrigerating Time: 4 hours

Top to bottom: Spiced Cranberry Orange Mold (page 154), Layered Cranberry Cheesecake (page 160), Holiday Poke Cake, Praline Pumpkin Pie (page 155)

Cranberry Fruit Mold

Experience delicious fruit-filled effervescence in this delightful mold!

> **2 cups boiling water**
> **1 package (8-serving size) or**
> **2 packages (4-serving size) JELL-O Brand Cranberry Flavor Gelatin Dessert or JELL-O Brand Cranberry Flavor Sugar Free Low Calorie Gelatin Dessert**
> **1½ cups cold ginger ale, lemon-lime carbonated beverage, seltzer or water**
> **2 cups halved green and/or red seedless grapes**
> **1 can (11 ounces) mandarin orange segments, drained**

STIR boiling water into gelatin in large bowl at least 2 minutes until completely dissolved. Stir in cold ginger ale. Refrigerate about 1½ hours or until thickened (spoon drawn through leaves definite impression). Stir in fruit. Spoon into 6-cup mold.

REFRIGERATE 4 hours or until firm. Unmold. Garnish as desired.

Makes 10 servings

 Nutrition Information Per Serving (using JELL-O Brand Cranberry Flavor Sugar Free Low Calorie Gelatin Dessert and seltzer and omitting garnish): 45 calories, 0g fat, 0mg cholesterol, 65mg sodium, 10g carbohydrate, less than 1g dietary fiber, 8g sugars, 2g protein, 20% daily vitamin C

Preparation Time: 15 minutes
Refrigerating Time: 5½ hours

Three little kittens took off their mittens
Enchanted, delighted and merry.
For each was to savor a new Jell-O flavor—
Black Raspberry, Grape and Black Cherry.

1956

Cranberry Fruit Mold

Merry Cherry Holiday Dessert

An easy yet spectacular finale to any holiday meal.

Speed-scratch cooking has really taken hold in the 1990's. This recipe is a fine example of achieving great results with convenience products. After all, JELL-O was one of the first convenience products available.

1½ cups boiling water
1 package (8-serving size) or 2 packages (4-serving size) JELL-O Brand Cherry Flavor Gelatin Dessert, or any red flavor
1½ cups cold water
1 can (21 ounces) cherry pie filling
4 cups angel food cake cubes
3 cups cold milk
2 packages (4-serving size) JELL-O Vanilla Flavor Instant Pudding & Pie Filling
1 tub (8 ounces) COOL WHIP Whipped Topping, thawed

STIR boiling water into gelatin in large bowl at least 2 minutes until completely dissolved. Stir in cold water and cherry pie filling. Refrigerate about 1 hour or until slightly thickened (consistency of unbeaten egg whites). Place cake cubes in 3-quart serving bowl. Spoon gelatin mixture over cake. Refrigerate about 45 minutes or until set but not firm (gelatin should stick to finger when touched and should mound).

POUR milk into large bowl. Add pudding mixes. Beat with wire whisk 1 minute. Gently stir in 2 cups of the whipped topping. Spoon over gelatin mixture in bowl.

REFRIGERATE 2 hours or until set. Top with remaining whipped topping and garnish as desired.

Makes 16 servings

Preparation Time: 20 minutes
Refrigerating Time: 3¾ hours

Merry Cherry Holiday Dessert

153

Spiced Cranberry Orange Mold

No holiday dinner should be without this!

Since its earliest days, JELL-O gelatin has been used as a "table jelly" to accompany meat and poultry. It is still prized for its delicious flavor and "delightful cooling quality."

1½ cups boiling water
1 package (8-serving size) or 2 packages (4-serving size) JELL-O Brand Cranberry Flavor Gelatin, or any red flavor
1 can (16 ounces) whole berry cranberry sauce
1 cup cold water
1 tablespoon lemon juice
¼ teaspoon ground cinnamon
⅛ teaspoon ground cloves
1 orange, sectioned, diced
½ cup chopped walnuts

STIR boiling water into gelatin in large bowl at least 2 minutes until completely dissolved. Stir in cranberry sauce, cold water, lemon juice, cinnamon and cloves. Refrigerate about 1½ hours or until thickened (spoon drawn through leaves definite impression).

STIR in orange and walnuts. Spoon into 5-cup mold.

REFRIGERATE 4 hours or until firm. Unmold. Garnish as desired.   *Makes 10 servings*

Preparation Time: 20 minutes
Refrigerating Time: 5½ hours

Praline Pumpkin Pie

The praline layer adds fabulous taste and texture to this Thanksgiving pie.

- ½ **cup chopped pecans or walnuts**
- ⅓ **cup butter or margarine**
- ⅓ **cup firmly packed brown sugar**
- 1 **prepared graham cracker crumb crust (6 ounces)**
- 1 **cup cold milk**
- 1 **can (16 ounces) pumpkin**
- 2 **packages (4-serving size) JELL-O Vanilla Flavor Instant Pudding & Pie Filling**
- 1¼ **teaspoons pumpkin pie spice**
- 1½ **cups thawed COOL WHIP Whipped Topping**

Traditional pumpkin pies bake for nearly an hour. This one takes only about 20 minutes to prepare and requires no baking at all!

BRING nuts, butter and sugar to boil in small saucepan on medium heat; boil 30 seconds. Spread onto bottom of crust. Cool.

POUR milk into large bowl. Add pumpkin, pudding mixes and spice. Beat with wire whisk until well mixed. (Mixture will be thick.) Immediately stir in whipped topping. Spread over nut layer.

REFRIGERATE 4 hours or until set. Garnish as desired.   *Makes 8 servings*

Preparation Time: 20 minutes
Refrigerating Time: 4 hours

JELL-O *Fun Facts*

Screen star Roy Rogers was the spokesman for JELL-O pudding in 1956.

"Red, White and Blue" Mold

First created in 1975, the "Red, White and Blue" Loaf recipe was revised in 1993 to include Berry Blue gelatin.

Dazzle the group on the Fourth of July with this festive molded salad!

2¾ cups boiling water
1 package (4-serving size) JELL-O Brand Strawberry Flavor Gelatin Dessert, or any red flavor
1 package (4-serving size) JELL-O Brand Berry Blue Flavor Gelatin Dessert
1 cup cold water
1½ cups sliced strawberries
1 package (4-serving size) JELL-O Brand Lemon Flavor Gelatin Dessert
1 pint (2 cups) vanilla ice cream, softened
1½ cups blueberries

STIR 1 cup of the boiling water into each of the red and blue gelatins in separate medium bowls at least 2 minutes until completely dissolved. Stir ½ cup of the cold water into each bowl.

PLACE bowl of red gelatin in larger bowl of ice and water. Stir until thickened, about 8 minutes. Stir in strawberries. Pour into 9×5-inch loaf pan. Refrigerate 7 minutes.

MEANWHILE, stir remaining ¾ cup boiling water into lemon gelatin in medium bowl at least 2 minutes until completely dissolved. Spoon in ice cream until melted and smooth. Spoon over red gelatin in pan. Refrigerate 7 minutes.

MEANWHILE, place bowl of blue gelatin in larger bowl of ice and water. Stir until thickened, about 7 minutes. Stir in blueberries. Spoon over lemon gelatin in pan.

REFRIGERATE 4 hours or until firm. Unmold. Garnish as desired.   *Makes 12 servings*

Preparing Time: 45 minutes
Refrigerating Time: 4½ hours

"Red, White and Blue" Mold

Luscious Lemon Poke Cake

Poke Cake first appeared in 1969. A huge hit with kids, it is one of the most requested JELL-O recipes. Here, white cake is a perfect foil for JELL-O gelatin's lively colors and flavors.

This refreshingly moist cake has a surprise for all inside!

2 baked 8- or 9-inch round white cake layers, cooled completely
2 cups boiling water
1 package (8-serving size) or 2 packages (4-serving size) JELL-O Brand Lemon Flavor Gelatin Dessert
1 tub (8 or 12 ounces) COOL WHIP Whipped Topping, thawed

PLACE cake layers, top sides up, in 2 clean 8- or 9-inch round cake pans. Pierce cake with large fork at ½-inch intervals.

STIR boiling water into gelatin in medium bowl at least 2 minutes until completely dissolved. Carefully pour 1 cup of the gelatin over 1 cake layer. Pour remaining gelatin over second cake layer. Refrigerate 3 hours.

DIP 1 cake pan in warm water 10 seconds; unmold onto serving plate. Spread with about 1 cup of the whipped topping. Unmold second cake layer; carefully place on first cake layer. Frost top and side of cake with remaining whipped topping.

REFRIGERATE at least 1 hour or until ready to serve. Decorate as desired.

Makes 12 servings

Preparation Time: 30 minutes
Refrigerating Time: 4 hours

Luscious Lemon Poke Cake

Layered Cranberry Cheesecake

Cheesecake dates back to Roman Empire days and still remains one of the most popular desserts of all time.

1 package (11.1 ounces) JELL-O No Bake Real Cheesecake
2 tablespoons sugar
⅓ cup butter or margarine, melted
1½ cups cold milk
½ cup whole berry cranberry sauce
¼ cup chopped walnuts, toasted

MIX crumbs, sugar and butter with fork in small bowl until crumbs are well moistened. Press firmly onto bottom of foil-lined 9-inch square pan.

BEAT milk and filling mix with electric mixer on low speed until well blended. Beat on medium speed 3 minutes. (Filling will be thick.) Spoon ½ of the filling over crust. Cover with cranberry sauce and walnuts. Top with remaining filling.

REFRIGERATE at least 1 hour. Garnish as desired.

Makes 9 servings

Preparation Time: 15 minutes
Refrigerating Time: 1 hour

Two fictional characters called Sammy, a boy, and Watson, his dog, introduced the concept of JELL-O Snacktivities in 1992. They were shown giving up fishing for an edible aquarium, spinning along on JELL-O pinwheels, and wolfing down Star Spangle Snacks on July 4th.

PHILADELPHIA

A Little Taste of

Heaven®

Appetizers, Cheesecakes & More

A Little Taste of **Heaven**®
Appetizers, Cheesecakes & More

Cheesecake Cream Dip

Prep: 5 minutes plus refrigerating

1 pkg. (8 oz.) PHILADELPHIA Cream Cheese, softened
1 jar (7 oz.) marshmallow cream

MIX cream cheese and marshmallow cream until well blended. Refrigerate.

SERVE with assorted cut-up fruit, pound cake or cookies.

Makes 1½ cups

Creamy Pesto Dip

Prep: 5 minutes plus refrigerating

> 1 pkg. (8 oz.) PHILADELPHIA Cream Cheese, softened
> 3 Tbsp. milk
> ⅓ cup DI GIORNO Basil Pesto
> 1 red pepper, finely chopped (about 1 cup)

MIX cream cheese and milk with electric mixer on medium speed until smooth. Blend in pesto and red pepper. Refrigerate.

SERVE with assorted cut-up vegetables, breadsticks or chips.

Makes about 2⅓ cups

Chili Cheese Dip

Prep: 5 minutes	*Microwave:* 3 minutes

> 1 pkg. (8 oz.) PHILADELPHIA Cream Cheese, softened
> 1 can (15 oz.) chili with or without beans
> 1 cup KRAFT Shredded Cheddar Cheese

SPREAD cream cheese onto bottom and up side of 9-inch microwavable pie plate or quiche dish. Spread chili over cream cheese. Sprinkle with cheddar cheese.

MICROWAVE on HIGH 3 minutes or until thoroughly heated.

SERVE with tortilla chips.

Makes 3 cups

Creamy Pesto Dip

Creamy Roasted Red Pepper Dip

Prep: 5 minutes plus refrigerating

> 1 pkg. (8 oz.) PHILADELPHIA Cream Cheese, softened
> 3 Tbsp. milk
> ½ cup roasted red peppers, drained, chopped
> ½ tsp. dried thyme leaves
> ⅛ tsp. ground black pepper

MIX cream cheese and milk with electric mixer on medium speed until smooth. Blend in remaining ingredients. Refrigerate.

SERVE with assorted cut-up vegetables.   *Makes 1½ cups*

Hot Crab Dip

Prep: 10 minutes   *Bake:* 30 minutes

> 2 pkg. (8 oz. each) PHILADELPHIA Cream Cheese, softened
> 2 cans (6 oz. each) crabmeat, rinsed, drained and flaked
> ½ cup KRAFT Shredded Parmesan Cheese
> ¼ cup chopped green onions
> 2 tsp. KRAFT Prepared Horseradish

MIX all ingredients with electric mixer on medium speed until well blended. Spoon into 9-inch pie plate or quiche dish.

BAKE at 350°F for 25 to 30 minutes or until very lightly browned.

SERVE with crackers.   *Makes 4 cups*

Creamy Roasted Red Pepper Dip

Hot Artichoke Dip

Prep: 15 minutes	*Bake:* 25 minutes

1 pkg. (8 oz.) PHILADELPHIA Cream Cheese, softened
1 can (14 oz.) artichoke hearts, drained, chopped
½ cup KRAFT Mayo Real Mayonnaise
½ cup KRAFT 100% Grated Parmesan Cheese
1 clove garlic, minced

MIX all ingredients with electric mixer on medium speed until well blended. Spoon into 9-inch pie plate or quiche dish.

BAKE at 350°F for 20 to 25 minutes or until very lightly browned.

SERVE with baked pita bread wedges or vegetable dippers.

Makes 2½ cups

Tip

Special Extras: To make baked pita bread wedges, cut each of 3 split pita breads into 8 triangles. Place on cookie sheet. Bake at 350°F for 10 to 12 minutes or until crisp. Makes 48 wedges.

Hot Artichoke Dip

Creamy Salsa Dip

Prep: 10 minutes plus refrigerating

1 pkg. (8 oz.) PHILADELPHIA Cream Cheese, softened 1 cup TACO BELL HOME ORIGINALS Salsa

MIX cream cheese and salsa until well blended. Refrigerate.

SERVE with tortilla chips or assorted cut-up vegetables.

Makes 2 cups

Spinach Dip

Prep: 10 minutes plus refrigerating

1 pkg. (8 oz.) PHILADELPHIA Cream Cheese, softened $\frac{1}{4}$ cup milk 1 pkg. (10 oz.) frozen chopped spinach, thawed, drained 1 can (8 oz.) water chestnuts, drained, chopped $\frac{1}{2}$ cup chopped red pepper $\frac{1}{2}$ tsp. garlic salt $\frac{1}{8}$ tsp. hot pepper sauce

MIX cream cheese and milk with electric mixer on medium speed until smooth. Blend in remaining ingredients. Refrigerate.

SERVE with assorted cut-up vegetables or potato chips.

Makes 3 cups

Creamy Salsa Dip

7-Layer Mexican Dip

Prep: 10 minutes plus refrigerating

1 pkg. (8 oz.) PHILADELPHIA Cream Cheese, softened
1 Tbsp. TACO BELL HOME ORIGINALS Taco Seasoning Mix
1 cup each guacamole, TACO BELL HOME ORIGINALS
    Salsa and shredded lettuce
1 cup KRAFT Shredded Mild Cheddar Cheese
½ cup chopped green onions
2 Tbsp. sliced pitted ripe olives

MIX cream cheese and seasoning mix. Spread onto bottom of 9-inch pie plate or quiche dish.

LAYER guacamole, salsa, lettuce, cheddar cheese, onions and olives over cream cheese mixture. Refrigerate.

SERVE with tortilla chips.   *Makes 6 to 8 servings*

Tip

Great Substitutes: *If your family doesn't like guacamole, try substituting 1 cup TACO BELL HOME ORIGINALS Refried Beans.*

7-Layer Mexican Dip

Baked Cream Cheese Appetizer

Prep: 10 minutes   *Bake:* 18 minutes

1 pkg. (4 oz.) refrigerated crescent dinner rolls
1 pkg. (8 oz.) PHILADELPHIA Cream Cheese
½ tsp. dill weed
1 egg white, beaten

UNROLL dough on lightly greased cookie sheet; press seams together to form 12×4-inch rectangle.

SPRINKLE cream cheese with dill; lightly press dill into cream cheese. Place cream cheese, dill-side up, in center of dough. Bring edges of dough up over cream cheese; press edges together to seal, completely enclosing cream cheese. Brush with egg white.

BAKE at 350°F for 15 to 18 minutes or until lightly browned. Serve with crackers, French bread or cut-up vegetables.   *Makes 8 servings*

Party Cheese Wreath

Prep: 15 minutes plus refrigerating

2 pkg. (8 oz. each) PHILADELPHIA Cream Cheese, softened
1 pkg. (8 oz.) KRAFT Shredded Sharp Cheddar Cheese
1 Tbsp. <u>each</u> chopped red bell pepper and finely chopped
    onion
2 tsp. Worcestershire sauce
1 tsp. lemon juice
    Dash ground red pepper

MIX cream cheese and Cheddar cheese with electric mixer on medium speed until well blended.

BLEND in remaining ingredients. Refrigerate several hours or overnight.

PLACE drinking glass in center of serving platter. Drop rounded tablespoonfuls of cheese mixture around glass, just touching outer edge of glass to form ring; smooth with spatula. Remove glass. Serve with crackers.   *Makes 12 servings*

Variation

Mini Cheese Balls: *Shape cream cheese mixture
into 1-inch balls. Roll in light rye bread crumbs or
dark pumpernickel bread crumbs.*

Party Cheese Wreath

Creamy Feta & Sun-Dried Tomato Spread

Prep: 10 minutes plus refrigerating

1 pkg. (8 oz.) PHILADELPHIA Cream Cheese, softened
1 pkg. (4 oz.) ATHENOS Crumbled Feta Cheese
2 Tbsp. chopped fresh basil
2 Tbsp. finely chopped sun-dried tomatoes

MIX all ingredients. Refrigerate.

SERVE with crackers or fresh vegetables.

Makes 1½ cups

Zesty Shrimp Spread

Prep: 5 minutes plus refrigerating

1 pkg. (8 oz.) PHILADELPHIA Cream Cheese, softened
½ cup KRAFT Mayo Real Mayonnaise
1 cup chopped, cooked, cleaned shrimp
¼ cup KRAFT 100% Grated Parmesan Cheese
2 Tbsp. chopped fresh parsley <u>or</u> cilantro
2 cloves garlic, minced

BEAT cream cheese and mayo with electric mixer on medium speed until well blended.

ADD remaining ingredients; mix well. Refrigerate.

SERVE with crackers or toasted bread rounds.

Makes 2¼ cups

Creamy Feta & Sun-Dried Tomato Spread

Three Pepper Quesadillas

Prep: 20 minutes	*Bake:* 8 minutes

1 cup <u>each</u> thin green, red and yellow pepper strips
½ cup thin onion slices
½ tsp. ground cumin
⅓ cup butter <u>or</u> margarine
1 pkg. (8 oz.) PHILADELPHIA Cream Cheese, softened
1 pkg. (8 oz.) KRAFT Shredded Sharp Cheddar Cheese
10 flour tortillas (6 inch)
  TACO BELL HOME ORIGINALS Salsa

COOK and stir peppers, onion and cumin in butter in large skillet 4 minutes or until vegetables are tender-crisp. Drain, reserving butter.

MIX cream cheese and Cheddar cheese until well blended. Spoon 2 Tbsp. cheese mixture onto each tortilla; top with scant ⅓ cup vegetable mixture. Fold tortillas in half; place on cookie sheet. Brush with reserved butter.

BAKE at 425°F for 8 minutes. Cut each tortilla into thirds. Serve warm with salsa.   *Makes 30 appetizers*

Three Pepper Quesadillas

No-Bake Inspirations

Cherries in the Snow

Prep: 10 minutes

---

1 pkg. (8 oz.) PHILADELPHIA Cream Cheese, softened
½ cup sugar
2 cups thawed COOL WHIP Whipped Topping
1 can (20 oz.) cherry pie filling, divided

MIX cream cheese and sugar in large bowl until smooth. Gently stir in whipped topping.

LAYER ¼ cup cream cheese mixture and 2 Tbsp. pie filling in each of 4 dessert bowls. Repeat layers. *Makes 4 servings*

Fluffy 2-Step Cheesecake

Prep: 15 minutes plus refrigerating

---

2 pkg. (8 oz. each) PHILADELPHIA Cream Cheese, softened
1/3 cup sugar
1 tub (8 oz.) COOL WHIP Whipped Topping, thawed
1 ready-to-use graham cracker crumb crust (6 oz. or 9 inch)

MIX cream cheese and sugar in large bowl with electric mixer on medium speed until smooth. Gently stir in whipped topping.

SPOON into crust. Refrigerate 3 hours or until set. Top with fresh fruit or cherry pie filling, if desired. Store leftover cheesecake in refrigerator.
Makes 8 servings

Chocolate Fudge

Prep: 15 minutes plus refrigerating

---

4 cups sifted powdered sugar
1 pkg. (8 oz.) PHILADELPHIA Cream Cheese, softened
4 squares BAKER'S Unsweetened Baking Chocolate, melted
1/2 cup chopped nuts
1 tsp. vanilla

ADD sugar gradually to cream cheese, beating with electric mixer on medium speed until well blended. Mix in remaining ingredients.

SPREAD into greased 8-inch square pan. Refrigerate several hours.

CUT into 1-inch squares. Refrigerate leftover fudge.
Makes 64 squares

Fluffy 2-Step Cheesecake

Easy English Trifle

Prep: 15 minutes plus refrigerating

1 pkg. (8 oz.) PHILADELPHIA Cream Cheese, softened
2 cups milk, divided
1 pkg. (4-serving size) JELL-O Vanilla Flavor Instant Pudding
    & Pie Filling
2½ cups cubed pound cake
½ cup strawberry preserves
1 can (16 oz.) peach slices, drained, chopped

MIX cream cheese and ½ cup of the milk with electric mixer on medium speed until well blended. Add pudding mix and remaining 1½ cups milk; beat on low speed 1 minute.

LAYER ½ each of the cake, preserves, peach slices and pudding mixture in 1½-quart serving bowl; repeat layers. Cover surface with wax paper or plastic wrap; refrigerate. *Makes 8 servings*

Chocolate Raspberry Cheesecake

Prep: 10 minutes plus refrigerating

½ cup raspberry fruit spread
1 ready-to-use graham cracker crumb crust (6 oz. or 9 inch)
2 pkg. (8 oz. each) PHILADELPHIA Cream Cheese, softened
1¼ cups chocolate flavored dessert topping
1 tub (8 oz.) COOL WHIP Whipped Topping, thawed

SPREAD fruit spread onto bottom of crust.

MIX cream cheese and dessert topping with electric mixer on medium speed until smooth. Gently stir in whipped topping.

SPOON over fruit spread in crust. Refrigerate 3 hours or until set. Drizzle with additional dessert topping, if desired.

Makes 8 servings

Easy English Trifle

KRAFT PHILADELPHIA

Heavenly Cheesecakes

Brownie Bottom Cheesecake

Prep: 20 minutes plus refrigerating   *Bake:* 65 minutes

---

1 pkg. (10 to 16 oz.) brownie mix, any variety (8×8-inch pan size)
3 pkg. (8 oz. each) PHILADELPHIA Cream Cheese, softened
¾ cup sugar
1 tsp. vanilla
½ cup BREAKSTONE'S <u>or</u> KNUDSEN Sour Cream
3 eggs

PREPARE and bake brownie mix as directed on package for 8-inch square pan in well-greased 9-inch springform pan.

MIX cream cheese, sugar and vanilla with electric mixer on medium speed until well blended. Blend in sour cream. Add eggs, mixing on low speed just until blended. Pour over brownie crust.

BAKE at 325°F for 60 to 65 minutes or until center is almost set if using a silver springform pan. (Bake at 300°F for 60 to 65 minutes or until center is almost set if using a dark nonstick springform pan.) Run knife or metal spatula around rim of pan to loosen cake; cool before removing rim of pan. Refrigerate 4 hours or overnight.

Makes 12 servings

Classic New York Cheesecake

Prep: 15 minutes plus refrigerating   *Bake:* 70 minutes

Crust
- 1 cup graham cracker crumbs
- 3 Tbsp. sugar
- 3 Tbsp. butter <u>or</u> margarine, melted

Filling
- 4 pkg. (8 oz. each) PHILADELPHIA Cream Cheese, softened
- 1 cup sugar
- 3 Tbsp. flour
- 1 Tbsp. vanilla
- 1 cup BREAKSTONE'S <u>or</u> KNUDSEN Sour Cream
- 4 eggs

Crust

MIX crumbs, sugar and butter; press onto bottom of 9-inch springform pan. Bake at 325°F for 10 minutes if using a silver springform pan. (Bake at 300°F for 10 minutes if using a dark nonstick springform pan.)

Filling

MIX cream cheese, sugar, flour and vanilla with electric mixer on medium speed until well blended. Blend in sour cream. Add eggs, mixing on low speed just until blended. Pour over crust.

BAKE at 325°F for 65 to 70 minutes or until center is almost set if using a 9-inch silver springform pan. (Bake at 300°F for 65 to 70 minutes or until center is almost set if using a 9-inch dark nonstick springform pan.) Run knife or metal spatula around rim of pan to loosen cake; cool before removing rim of pan. Refrigerate 4 hours or overnight.   *Makes 12 servings*

Classic New York Cheesecake

Tips from the Kraft Kitchens

For great cheesecakes, follow these quick mixing and baking tips:

Mixing:

- Soften PHILADELPHIA Cream Cheese before mixing. To soften in microwave, place an unwrapped (8 oz.) pkg. in microwavable bowl. Microwave on HIGH 15 seconds. Add 15 seconds for each additional package.

- Don't overbeat. Beat at low speed after adding eggs, just until blended.

Baking:

- Don't peek into the oven during baking.

- Don't overbake. When done, edges should be slightly puffed. The center area, about the size of a silver dollar, should still appear soft and moist. The center will firm upon cooling.

Cooling:

- Cool cheesecake on wire rack at room temperature for 1 hour before refrigerating.

- Refrigerate, uncovered, 3 to 4 hours or until thoroughly chilled. Place sheet of plastic wrap or foil over top of cheesecake; secure. Refrigerate overnight or up to 2 days.

Freezing:

- Prepare cheesecake as directed, omitting any topping. Wrap securely in plastic wrap; overwrap with foil. Place in plastic bag and seal. Freeze up to 2 months.

- Thaw wrapped cheesecake in refrigerator overnight.

Easy Steps Toward Success:

Crust:

• For baked springform pan cheesecakes, prepare crust by pressing crust mixture into pan. A mixture of graham cracker crumbs, sugar and melted butter or margarine is shown here.

Loosening Cheesecake from Pan:

• Immediately upon removal from oven, run a thin metal spatula or knife around edge of cheesecake (pushing against side of pan) to loosen it from side of pan. Keep spring fastener on side of pan locked and springform side on. Cool 1 hour at room temperature; refrigerate.

Removing Pan:

• Loosen spring fastener. Lift rim of pan straight up to separate it from cheesecake.

KRAFT
kitchens

Double Lemon Cheesecake

Prep: 35 minutes plus refrigerating   *Bake:* 55 minutes

Crust
   1 cup vanilla wafer cookie crumbs
   3 Tbsp. sugar
   3 Tbsp. butter <u>or</u> margarine, melted

Filling
   3 pkg. (8 oz. each) PHILADELPHIA Cream Cheese, softened
   1 cup sugar
   3 Tbsp. flour
   2 Tbsp. lemon juice
   1 Tbsp. grated lemon peel
   ½ tsp. vanilla
   3 eggs
   1 egg white

Topping
   ¾ cup sugar
   2 Tbsp. cornstarch
   ½ cup water
   ¼ cup lemon juice
   1 egg yolk, beaten

Crust
MIX crumbs, sugar and butter; press onto bottom of 9-inch springform pan. Bake at 325°F for 10 minutes if using a silver springform pan. (Bake at 300°F for 10 minutes if using a dark nonstick springform pan).

Filling
MIX cream cheese, sugar, flour, juice, peel and vanilla with electric mixer on medium speed until well blended. Add 3 eggs and egg white, mixing on low speed just until blended. Pour over crust.

Continued on page 202

Double Lemon Cheesecake

Double Lemon Cheesecake, continued

BAKE at 325°F for 50 to 55 minutes or until center is almost set if using a silver springform pan. (Bake at 300°F for 50 to 55 minutes or until center is almost set if using a dark nonstick springform pan). Run knife or metal spatula around rim of pan to loosen cake; cool before removing rim of pan. Refrigerate 4 hours or overnight.

Topping
MIX sugar and cornstarch in saucepan; gradually stir in water and juice. Bring mixture to low boil on medium heat, stirring constantly until clear and thickened. Stir 2 tablespoons of the hot mixture into egg yolks; return to hot mixture. Cook 1 minute or until thickened, stirring constantly. Cool slightly. Spoon topping over cheesecake; refrigerate.   *Makes 12 servings*

Tip

Great Substitutes: *You can substitute 1 jar of prepared lemon curd from a specialty food store for lemon topping.*

Amaretto Macaroon Cheesecake

Prep: 25 minutes plus refrigerating   *Bake:* 1 hour

Crust
   1 pkg. (7 oz.) BAKER'S ANGEL FLAKE Coconut, lightly
      toasted
   ½ cup finely chopped lightly toasted almonds
   1 can (14 oz.) sweetened condensed milk, divided
   ⅓ cup flour
   ¼ cup (½ stick) butter *or* margarine, melted

Filling
   4 pkg. (8 oz. each) PHILADELPHIA Cream Cheese, softened
   ¼ cup sugar
   ¼ cup almond-flavored liqueur
   4 eggs

Crust
MIX coconut, almonds, ½ cup of the sweetened condensed milk,
flour and butter; press onto bottom of greased 9-inch springform pan.

Filling
MIX cream cheese, sugar and remaining ¾ cup sweetened condensed
milk with electric mixer on medium speed until well blended. Blend
in liqueur. Add eggs, mixing on low speed just until blended. Pour
over crust.

BAKE at 325°F for 55 to 60 minutes or until center is almost set if
using a silver springform pan. (Bake at 300°F for 55 to 60 minutes or
until center is almost set if using a dark nonstick springform pan.)
Run knife or metal spatula around rim of pan to loosen cake; cool
before removing rim of pan. Refrigerate 4 hours or overnight.

Makes 12 servings

Café Latte Cheesecake

Prep: 25 minutes plus refrigerating   *Bake:* 65 minutes

Crust
  1 cup vanilla wafer cookie crumbs
  3 Tbsp. sugar
  3 Tbsp. butter <u>or</u> margarine, melted

Filling
  4 pkg. (8 oz. each) PHILADELPHIA Cream Cheese, softened
  1 cup sugar
  1 Tbsp. vanilla
  4 eggs
  3 Tbsp. milk
  3 Tbsp. MAXWELL HOUSE Instant Coffee
  1 Tbsp. warm water

Crust
MIX crumbs, sugar and butter; press onto bottom of 9-inch springform pan. Bake at 325°F for 10 minutes if using a silver springform pan. (Bake at 300°F for 10 minutes if using a dark nonstick springform pan.)

Filling
MIX cream cheese, sugar and vanilla with electric mixer on medium speed until well blended. Add eggs, mixing on low speed just until blended. Reserve 1½ cups of the batter. Stir instant coffee into warm water until dissolved. Add to remaining batter; mix well. Pour over crust. Stir milk into reserved batter; pour gently over coffee batter.

BAKE at 325°F for 65 minutes or until center is almost set if using a sliver springform pan. (Bake at 300°F for 65 minutes or until center is almost set if using a dark nonstick springform pan.) Run knife or metal spatula around rim of pant to loosen cake; cool before removing rim of pan. Refrigerate 4 hours or overnight.

Makes 12 servings

Café Latte Cheesecake

Chocolate Mint Swirl Cheesecake

Prep: 25 minutes plus refrigerating   *Bake:* 1 hour

Crust
  1 cup chocolate wafer cookie crumbs
  3 Tbsp. sugar
  3 Tbsp. butter <u>or</u> margarine, melted

Filling
  4 pkg. (8 oz. each) PHILADELPHIA Cream Cheese, softened
  1 cup sugar
  1 tsp. vanilla
  4 eggs
  2 squares BAKER'S Semi-Sweet Baking Chocolate, melted
  1 pkg. (4.67 oz.) crème de menthe candies, coarsely chopped
10 drops green food coloring

Crust
MIX crumbs, sugar and butter; press onto bottom of 9-inch springform pan. Bake at 325°F for 10 minutes if using a silver springform pan. (Bake at 300°F for 10 minutes if using a dark nonstick springform pan.)

Filling
MIX cream cheese, sugar and vanilla with electric mixer on medium speed until well blended. Add eggs, mixing on low speed just until blended. Spoon 1½ cups batter into small bowl; blend in melted chocolate. Add mint candies and food coloring to remaining batter. Pour ½ of the mint batter over crust. Using tablespoon, dollop ½ of the chocolate batter over mint batter layer; repeat layers. Cut through batter with knife several times to create marble effect.

BAKE at 325°F for 1 hour or until center is almost set if using a silver springform pan. (Bake at 300°F for 1 hour or until center is almost set if using a dark nonstick springform pan.) Run knife or metal spatula around rim of pan to loosen cake; cool before removing rim of pan. Refrigerate 4 hours or overnight.   *Makes 12 servings*

Chocolate Mint Swirl Cheesecake

Pumpkin Marble Cheesecake

Prep: 25 minutes plus refrigerating   *Bake:* 55 minutes

Crust
- 2 cups gingersnap cookie crumbs
- ½ cup finely chopped pecans
- 6 Tbsp. butter <u>or</u> margarine, melted

Filling
- 3 pkg. (8 oz. each) PHILADELPHIA Cream Cheese, softened
- 1 cup sugar, divided
- 1 tsp. vanilla
- 3 eggs
- 1 cup canned pumpkin
- 1 tsp. ground cinnamon
- ¼ tsp. ground nutmeg
- Dash ground cloves

Crust

MIX crumbs, pecans and butter; press onto bottom and 2 inches up side of 9-inch springform pan.

Filling

MIX cream cheese, ¾ cup of the sugar and vanilla with electric mixer on medium speed until well blended. Add eggs, mixing on low speed just until blended. Reserve 1½ cups batter. Add remaining ¼ cup sugar, pumpkin and spices to remaining batter; mix well. Spoon ½ of the pumpkin batter over crust; top with spoonfuls of plain batter. Repeat layers. Cut through batter with knife several times for marble effect.

BAKE at 325°F for 55 minutes or until center is almost set if using a silver springform pan. (Bake at 300°F for 55 minutes or until center is almost set if using a dark nonstick springform pan.) Run knife or metal spatula around rim of pan to loosen cake; cool before removing rim of pan. Refrigerate 4 hours or overnight.   *Makes 12 servings*

Pumpkin Marble Cheesecake

PHILADELPHIA® 3-STEP® Cheesecake

Prep: 10 minutes plus refrigerating	*Bake:* 40 minutes

2 pkg. (8 oz. each) PHILADELPHIA Cream Cheese, softened
½ cup sugar
½ tsp. vanilla
2 eggs
1 ready-to-use graham cracker crumb crust (6 oz. or 9 inch)

MIX cream cheese, sugar and vanilla with electric mixer on medium speed until well blended. Add eggs; mix until blended.

POUR into crust.

BAKE at 350°F for 40 minutes or until center is almost set. Cool. Refrigerate 3 hours or overnight.   *Makes 8 servings*

PHILADELPHIA® 3-STEP® Lime Cheesecake

Prep: 10 minutes plus refrigerating	*Bake:* 40 minutes

> 2 pkg. (8 oz. each) PHILADELPHIA Cream Cheese, softened
> ½ cup sugar
> 2 Tbsp. fresh lime juice
> 1 tsp. grated lime peel
> ½ tsp. vanilla
> 2 eggs
> 1 ready-to-use graham cracker crust (6 oz. or 9 inch)

MIX cream cheese, sugar, juice, peel and vanilla with electric mixer on medium speed until well blended. Add eggs; mix until blended.

POUR into crust.

BAKE at 350°F for 35 to 40 minutes or until center is almost set. Cool. Refrigerate 3 hours or overnight.   *Makes 8 servings*

Variation

Lemon Cheesecake: Prepare as directed, substituting 1 Tbsp. fresh lemon juice for lime juice and ½ tsp. grated lemon peel for lime peel.

PHILADELPHIA® 3-STEP® Chocolate Swirl Cheesecake

Prep: 10 minutes plus refrigerating	*Bake:* 40 minutes

 2 pkg. (8 oz. each) PHILADELPHIA Cream Cheese, softened
½ cup sugar
½ tsp. vanilla
 2 eggs
 1 square BAKER'S Semi-Sweet Baking Chocolate, melted, slightly cooled
 1 ready-to-use chocolate flavor crumb crust (6 oz. or 9 inch)

MIX cream cheese, sugar and vanilla with electric mixer on medium speed until well blended. Add eggs; mix until blended. Stir melted chocolate into ¾ cup of the cream cheese batter.

POUR remaining cream cheese batter into crust. Spoon chocolate batter over cream cheese batter; cut through batter with knife several times for marble effect.

BAKE at 350°F for 35 to 40 minutes or until center is almost set. Cool. Refrigerate 3 hours or overnight.   *Makes 8 servings*

PHILADELPHIA® 3-STEP® Caramel Pecan Cheesecake

Prep: 15 minutes plus refrigerating	*Bake:* 40 minutes

20 caramels
3 Tbsp. milk
½ cup chopped pecans
1 ready-to-use graham cracker crumb crust (6 oz. or 9 inch)
2 pkg. (8 oz. each) PHILADELPHIA Cream Cheese, softened
½ cup sugar
½ tsp. vanilla
2 eggs

MICROWAVE caramels and milk in small bowl on HIGH 2 minutes or until smooth, stirring every minute. Stir in pecans; pour into crust. Refrigerate 10 minutes.

MIX cream cheese, sugar and vanilla with electric mixer on medium speed until well blended. Add eggs; mix until blended. Pour over caramel mixture.

BAKE at 350°F for 35 to 40 minutes or until center is almost set. Cool. Refrigerate 3 hours or overnight. Garnish with pecan halves and caramel sauce.   *Makes 8 servings*

PHILADELPHIA® 3-STEP® White Chocolate Raspberry Swirl Cheesecake

Prep: 10 minutes plus refrigerating   *Bake:* 40 minutes

2 pkg. (8 oz. each) PHILADELPHIA Cream Cheese, softened
½ cup sugar
½ tsp. vanilla
2 eggs
3 squares (3 oz.) BAKER'S Premium White Baking Chocolate, melted
1 ready-to-use chocolate flavor crumb crust (6 oz. or 9 inch)
3 Tbsp. red raspberry preserves

MIX cream cheese, sugar and vanilla with electric mixer on medium speed until well blended. Add eggs; mix until blended. Stir in white chocolate.

POUR into crust. Microwave preserves in small bowl on HIGH 15 seconds or until melted. Dot top of cheesecake with small spoonfuls of preserves. Cut through batter with knife several times for swirl effect.

BAKE at 350°F for 35 to 40 minutes or until center is almost set. Cool. Refrigerate 3 hours or overnight.   *Makes 8 servings*

PHILADELPHIA® 3-STEP® Triple Chocolate Layer Cheesecake

Prep: 10 minutes plus refrigerating   *Bake:* 40 minutes

2 pkg. (8 oz. each) PHILADELPHIA Cream Cheese, softened
½ cup sugar
½ tsp. vanilla
2 eggs
3 squares BAKER'S Semi-Sweet Baking Chocolate, melted, slightly cooled
4 squares BAKER'S Premium White Baking Chocolate, melted, slightly cooled
1 ready-to-use chocolate flavor crumb crust (6 oz. or 9 inch)

MIX cream cheese, sugar and vanilla with electric mixer on medium speed until well blended. Add eggs; mix until blended. Stir melted semi-sweet chocolate into 1 cup of the batter. Stir melted white chocolate into remaining plain batter.

POUR semi-sweet chocolate batter into crust. Top with white chocolate batter.

BAKE at 350°F for 35 to 40 minutes or until center is almost set. Cool. Refrigerate 3 hours or overnight.   *Makes 8 servings*

220

PHILADELPHIA® 3-STEP® Cappuccino Cheesecake

Prep: 10 minutes plus refrigerating   *Bake:* 40 minutes

2 pkg. (8 oz. each) PHILADELPHIA Cream Cheese, softened
½ cup sugar
½ tsp. vanilla
2 eggs
1 Tbsp. milk
2 Tbsp. MAXWELL HOUSE Instant Coffee
1 ready-to-use chocolate crumb crust (6 oz. or 9 inch)

MIX cream cheese, sugar and vanilla with electric mixer on medium speed until well blended. Add eggs; mix until blended.

MICROWAVE milk on HIGH 15 seconds. Stir instant coffee into milk until dissolved. Stir into batter. Pour into crust.

BAKE at 350°F for 35 to 40 minutes or until center is almost set. Cool. Refrigerate 3 hours or overnight.   *Makes 8 servings*

Tip

Special Extras: *When serving cheesecake, wipe knife blade with a damp cloth between each slice for clean edges.*

221

PHILADELPHIA® 3-STEP® Black Forest Cherry Cheesecake

Prep: 10 minutes plus refrigerating	*Bake:* 40 minutes

> 2 pkg. (8 oz. each) PHILADELPHIA Cream Cheese, softened
> ½ cup sugar
> ½ tsp. vanilla
> 2 eggs
> 4 squares BAKER'S Semi-Sweet Baking Chocolate, melted, slightly cooled
> 1 ready-to-use chocolate flavor crumb crust (6 oz. or 9 inch)
> 1 cup thawed COOL WHIP Whipped Topping
> 1 cup cherry pie filling

MIX cream cheese, sugar and vanilla with electric mixer on medium speed until well blended. Add eggs; mix until blended. Stir in melted chocolate.

POUR into crust.

BAKE at 350°F for 35 to 40 minutes or until center is almost set. Cool. Refrigerate 3 hours or overnight. Spread whipped topping over chilled cheesecake; cover with pie filling.   *Makes 8 servings*

PHILADELPHIA® 3-STEP® Toffee Crunch Cheesecake

Prep: 10 minutes plus refrigerating   *Bake:* 40 minutes

2 pkg. (8 oz. each) PHILADELPHIA Cream Cheese, softened
½ cup firmly packed brown sugar
½ tsp. vanilla
2 eggs
4 pkg. (1.4 oz. each) chocolate-covered English toffee bars, chopped (1 cup), divided
1 ready-to-use graham cracker crumb crust (6 oz. or 9 inch)

MIX cream cheese, sugar and vanilla with electric mixer on medium speed until well blended. Add eggs; mix until blended. Stir in ¾ cup of the chopped toffee bars.

POUR into crust. Sprinkle with remaining toffee bars.

BAKE at 350°F for 35 to 40 minutes or until center is almost set. Cool. Refrigerate 3 hours or overnight.   *Makes 8 servings*

Tip

Make Your Own Crust: Mix 1⅓ cups graham cracker crumbs, 3 Tbsp. sugar and ⅓ cup butter or margarine, melted. Firmly press onto bottom and up side of 9-inch pie plate. Pour cheesecake batter into unbaked crust.

PHILADELPHIA® 3-STEP® Pumpkin Layer Cheesecake

Prep: 10 minutes plus refrigerating   *Bake:* 40 minutes

2 pkg. (8 oz. each) PHILADELPHIA Cream Cheese, softened
½ cup sugar
½ tsp. vanilla
2 eggs
½ cup canned pumpkin
½ tsp. ground cinnamon
    Dash <u>each</u> ground cloves and nutmeg
1 ready-to-use graham cracker crumb crust (6 oz. or 9 inch)

MIX cream cheese, sugar and vanilla with electric mixer on medium speed until well blended. Add eggs; mix until blended.

STIR pumpkin and spices into 1 cup of the batter; pour remaining plain batter into crust. Top with pumpkin batter.

BAKE at 350°F for 35 to 40 minutes or until center is almost set. Cool. Refrigerate 3 hours or overnight. Store leftover cheesecake in refrigerator.   *Makes 8 servings*

Blissful Bars & Cookies

Holiday Cheesecake Presents

Prep: 10 minutes plus refrigerating   *Bake:* 30 minutes

1½ **cups graham cracker crumbs**
⅓ **cup butter <u>or</u> margarine, melted**
3 **Tbsp. sugar**
3 **pkg. (8 oz. each) PHILADELPHIA Cream Cheese, softened**
¾ **cup sugar**
1 **tsp. vanilla**
3 **eggs**

MIX crumbs, butter and 3 Tbsp. sugar; press onto bottom of 13✕9-inch baking pan.

MIX cream cheese, ¾ cup sugar and vanilla with electric mixer on medium speed until well blended. Add eggs; mix until blended. Pour over crust.

BAKE at 350°F for 30 minutes or until center is almost set. Cool. Refrigerate 3 hours or overnight. Cut into bars. Decorate bars with decorating gels and sprinkles to resemble presents. Store leftover bars in refrigerator.   *Makes 2 dozen*

PHILADELPHIA® Snowmen Cookies

Prep: 20 minutes   *Bake:* 21 minutes

1 pkg. (8 oz.) PHILADELPHIA Cream Cheese, softened
1 cup powdered sugar
¾ cup (1½ sticks) butter <u>or</u> margarine
½ tsp. vanilla
2¼ cups flour
½ tsp. baking soda
     Sifted powdered sugar
     Miniature peanut butter cups (optional)

MIX cream cheese, 1 cup sugar, butter and vanilla with electric mixer on medium speed until well blended. Add flour and baking soda; mix well.

SHAPE dough into equal number of ½-inch and 1-inch diameter balls. Using 1 small and 1 large ball for each snowman, place balls, slightly overlapping, on ungreased cookie sheets. Flatten to ¼-inch thickness with bottom of glass dipped in additional flour. Repeat with remaining balls.

BAKE at 325°F for 19 to 21 minutes or until light golden brown. Cool on wire racks. Sprinkle each snowman with sifted powdered sugar. Decorate with icing as desired. Cut peanut butter cups in half for hats.   *Makes about 3 dozen*

PHILADELPHIA® Snowmen Cookies

Frosted Pumpkin Squares

Prep: 20 minutes	*Bake:* 35 minutes

Cake
   ¾ cup (1½ sticks) butter <u>or</u> margarine
   2 cups granulated sugar
   1 can (16 oz.) pumpkin
   4 eggs
   2 cups flour
   2 tsp. CALUMET Baking Powder
   1 tsp. ground cinnamon
   ½ tsp. baking soda
   ½ tsp. salt
   ¼ tsp. ground nutmeg
   1 cup chopped walnuts

Frosting
   1 pkg. (8 oz.) PHILADELPHIA Cream Cheese, softened
   ⅓ cup butter <u>or</u> margarine
   1 tsp. vanilla
   3 cups sifted powdered sugar

Cake

MIX butter and sugar with electric mixer on medium speed until light and fluffy. Blend in pumpkin and eggs. Mix in combined dry ingredients. Stir in walnuts.

SPREAD into greased and floured 15×10×1-inch baking pan.

BAKE at 350°F for 30 to 35 minutes or until wooden pick inserted in center comes out clean; cool.

Frosting

MIX cream cheese, butter and vanilla in large bowl with electric mixer until creamy. Gradually add sugar, mixing well after each addition. Spread onto cake. Cut into squares.   *Makes 2 dozen*

Frosted Pumpkin Squares

Creamy Lemon Bars

Prep: 15 minutes	*Bake:* 35 minutes

1 pkg. (2-layer size) lemon cake mix
3 large eggs, divided
½ cup oil
2 pkg. (8 oz. each) PHILADELPHIA Cream Cheese, softened
1 container (8 oz.) BREAKSTONE'S <u>or</u> KNUDSEN Sour Cream
½ cup granulated sugar
1 tsp. grated lemon peel
1 Tbsp. lemon juice
Powdered sugar

MIX cake mix, 1 egg and oil. Press mixture onto bottom and up sides of lightly greased 15×10×1-inch baking pan. Bake at 350°F for 10 minutes.

MIX cream cheese with electric mixer on medium speed until smooth. Add remaining 2 eggs, sour cream, granulated sugar, peel and juice; mix until blended. Pour batter into crust.

BAKE at 350°F for 30 to 35 minutes or until filling is just set in center and edges are light golden brown. Cool. Sprinkle with powdered sugar. Cut into bars. Store leftover bars in refrigerator.

Makes 2 dozen

Creamy Lemon Bars

PHILADELPHIA® Cheesecake Brownies

Prep: 20 minutes	*Bake:* 40 minutes

1 pkg. (19.8 oz.) brownie mix (do not use mix that includes syrup pouch)
1 pkg. (8 oz.) PHILADELPHIA Cream Cheese, softened
⅓ cup sugar
1 egg
½ tsp. vanilla

PREPARE brownie mix as directed on package. Pour into greased 13×9-inch baking pan.

MIX cream cheese with electric mixer on medium speed until smooth. Mix in sugar until blended. Add egg and vanilla; mix just until blended. Pour cream cheese mixture over brownie batter; cut through batter with knife several times for marble effect.

BAKE at 350°F for 35 to 40 minutes or until cream cheese mixture is lightly browned. Cool. Cut into squares.   *Makes 2 dozen*

PHILADELPHIA® Cheesecake Brownies

Choco-Cherry Bars

Prep: 30 minutes   *Bake:* 30 minutes

Bars
 1 pkg. (8 oz.) PHILADELPHIA Cream Cheese, softened
 ¾ cup (1½ sticks) butter <u>or</u> margarine, softened
 1 cup sugar
 2 eggs
 1 tsp. vanilla
1¼ cups flour
 ½ tsp. <u>each</u> baking soda and salt
 2 squares BAKER'S Unsweetened Baking Chocolate, melted
 1 cup chopped maraschino cherries, well drained
 ½ cup chopped walnuts

Glaze
 1 cup sifted powdered sugar
 3 Tbsp. milk
 2 squares BAKER'S Unsweetened Baking Chocolate, melted
 ½ tsp. vanilla

Bars
MIX cream cheese, butter and sugar with electric mixer on medium speed until well blended. Add eggs and vanilla; mix until blended.

MIX flour, baking soda and salt. Add flour mixture to cream cheese mixture; mix well. Blend in melted chocolate. Stir in cherries and walnuts. Spread into greased and floured 15×10×1-inch baking pan.

BAKE at 350°F for 25 to 30 minutes or until toothpick inserted in center comes out clean.

Glaze
MIX powdered sugar, milk, melted chocolate and vanilla until smooth. Drizzle over warm bars in baking pan; cut into bars.

Makes 2 dozen

My Favorites

My Favorite Recipes

Favorite recipe: _____

Favorite recipe from: _____

Ingredients: _____

_____

_____

_____

_____

_____

Method: _____

_____

_____

_____

_____

_____

_____

_____

_____

_____

_____

My Favorite Recipes

Favorite recipe: _____

Favorite recipe from: _____

Ingredients: _____

_____

_____

_____

_____

_____

Method: _____

_____

_____

_____

_____

_____

_____

_____

_____

_____

_____

_____

My Favorite Recipes

Favorite recipe: _____

Favorite recipe from: _____

Ingredients: _____

_____

_____

_____

_____

_____

Method: _____

_____

_____

_____

_____

_____

_____

_____

_____

My Favorite Recipes

Favorite recipe: _____

Favorite recipe from: _____

Ingredients: _____

_____

_____

_____

_____

_____

Method: _____

_____

_____

_____

_____

_____

_____

_____

_____

_____

_____

My Favorite Recipes

Favorite recipe: _____

Favorite recipe from: _____

Ingredients: _____

_____

_____

_____

_____

_____

Method: _____

_____

_____

_____

_____

_____

_____

_____

_____

_____

_____

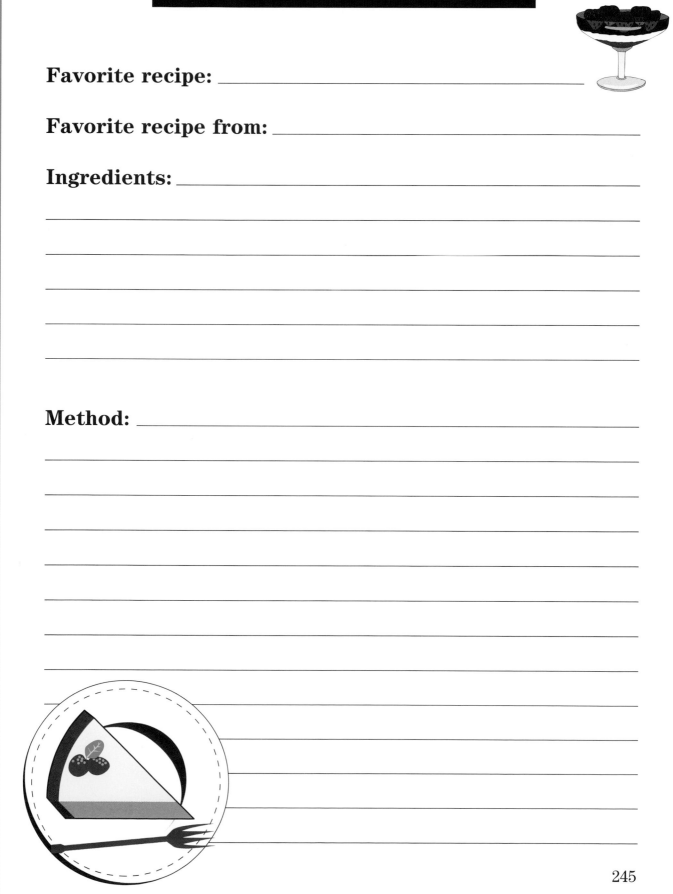

My Favorite Recipes

Favorite recipe: _____

Favorite recipe from: _____

Ingredients: _____

_____

_____

_____

_____

_____

Method: _____

_____

_____

_____

_____

_____

_____

_____

_____

_____

My Favorite Recipes

Favorite recipe: _____

Favorite recipe from: _____

Ingredients: _____

_____

_____

_____

_____

_____

Method: _____

_____

_____

_____

_____

_____

_____

_____

_____

_____

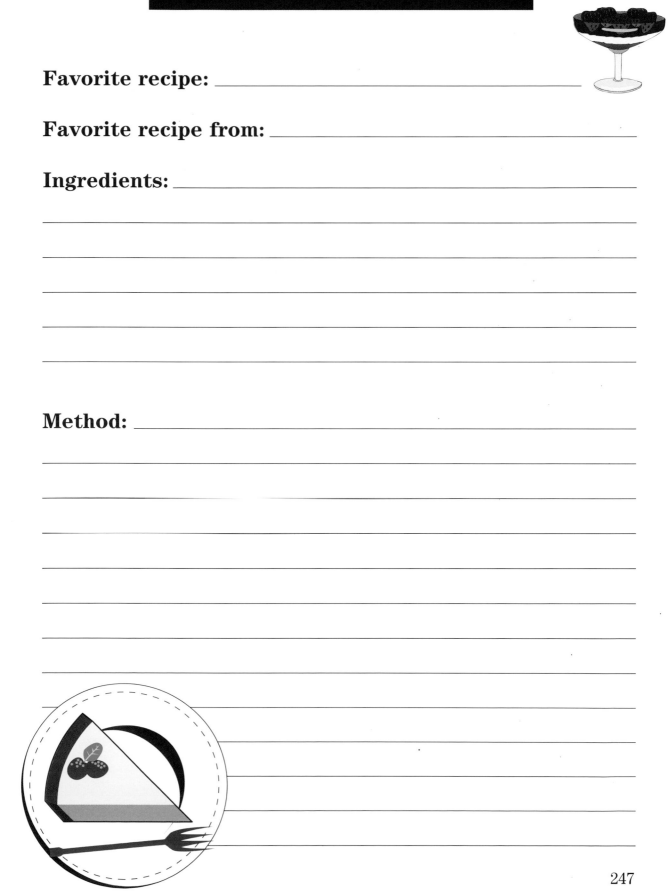

My Favorite Recipes

Favorite recipe: _____

Favorite recipe from: _____

Ingredients: _____

_____

_____

_____

_____

_____

Method: _____

_____

_____

_____

_____

_____

_____

_____

_____

_____

_____

My Favorite Recipes

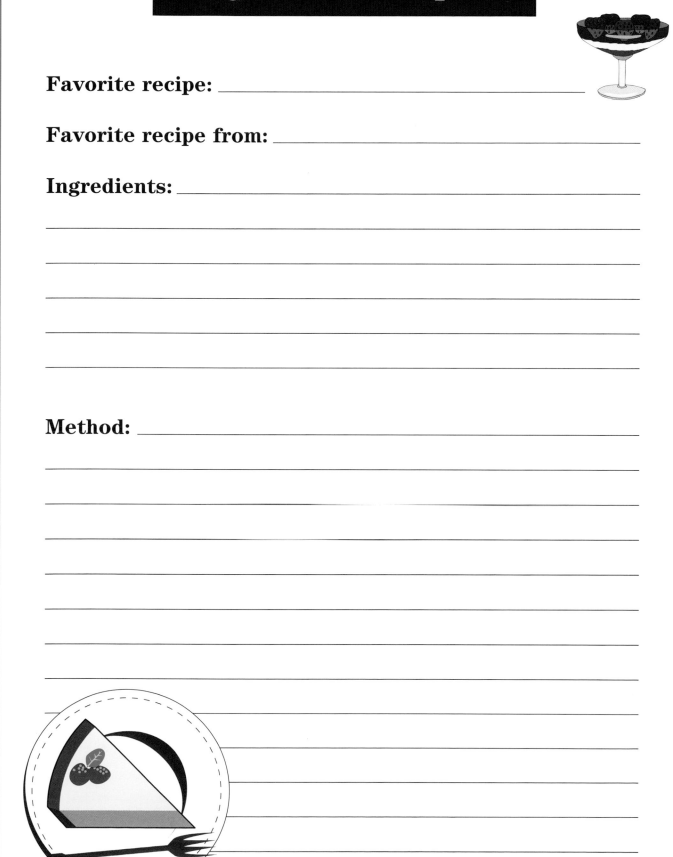

Favorite recipe: _____

Favorite recipe from: _____

Ingredients: _____

_____

_____

_____

_____

_____

Method: _____

_____

_____

_____

_____

_____

_____

_____

_____

_____

_____

My Favorite Recipes

Favorite recipe: _____

Favorite recipe from: _____

Ingredients: _____

_____

_____

_____

_____

_____

Method: _____

_____

_____

_____

_____

_____

_____

_____

_____

_____

_____

250

My Favorite Recipes

Favorite recipe: _____

Favorite recipe from: _____

Ingredients: _____

_____

_____

_____

_____

Method: _____

_____

_____

_____

_____

_____

_____

_____

_____

_____

Favorite recipe: _____

Favorite recipe from: _____

Ingredients: _____

_____

_____

_____

_____

_____

Method: _____

_____

_____

_____

_____

_____

_____

_____

_____

_____

_____

My Favorite Recipes

Favorite recipe: _____

Favorite recipe from: _____

Ingredients: _____

_____

_____

_____

_____

_____

Method: _____

_____

_____

_____

_____

_____

_____

_____

_____

_____

_____

Favorite recipe: _____

Favorite recipe from: _____

Ingredients: _____

_____

_____

_____

_____

_____

Method: _____

_____

_____

_____

_____

_____

_____

_____

_____

_____

_____

_____

My Favorite Recipes

Favorite recipe: _____

Favorite recipe from: _____

Ingredients: _____

_____

_____

_____

_____

_____

Method: _____

_____

_____

_____

_____

_____

_____

_____

_____

_____

_____

My Favorite Recipes

Favorite recipe: _____

Favorite recipe from: _____

Ingredients: _____

_____

_____

_____

_____

_____

Method: _____

_____

_____

_____

_____

_____

_____

_____

_____

_____

_____

_____

Favorite recipe: _____

Favorite recipe from: _____

Ingredients: _____

_____

_____

_____

_____

_____

Method: _____

_____

_____

_____

_____

_____

_____

_____

_____

_____

My Favorite Recipes

Favorite recipe: _____

Favorite recipe from: _____

Ingredients: _____

_____

_____

_____

_____

_____

Method: _____

_____

_____

_____

_____

_____

_____

_____

_____

_____

_____

_____

My Favorite Recipes

Favorite recipe: _____

Favorite recipe from: _____

Ingredients: _____

_____

_____

_____

_____

Method: _____

_____

_____

_____

_____

_____

_____

_____

_____

My Favorite Recipes

Favorite recipe: _____

Favorite recipe from: _____

Ingredients: _____

_____

_____

_____

_____

_____

Method: _____

_____

_____

_____

_____

_____

_____

_____

_____

_____

_____

_____

Favorite recipe: _____

Favorite recipe from: _____

Ingredients: _____

_____

_____

_____

_____

_____

Method: _____

_____

_____

_____

_____

_____

_____

_____

_____

_____

My Favorite Starters & Sides

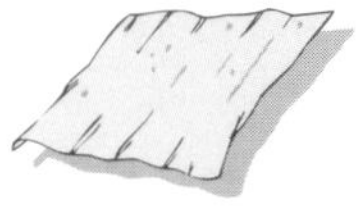

Date: ____________________

Occasion: ____________________

____

Guests: ____________________

____

____

____

____

Menu: ____________________

____

____

____

____

____

____

____

____

____

____

____

____

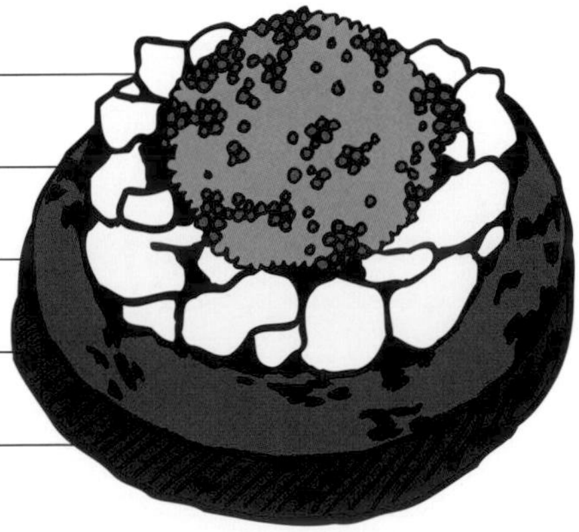

My Favorite Starters & Sides

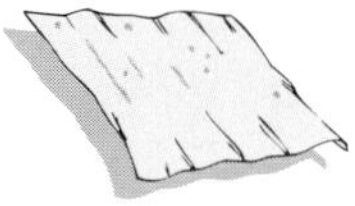

Date: _____

Occasion: _____
_____

Guests: _____
_____
_____
_____
_____

Menu: _____
_____
_____
_____
_____
_____
_____
_____
_____
_____

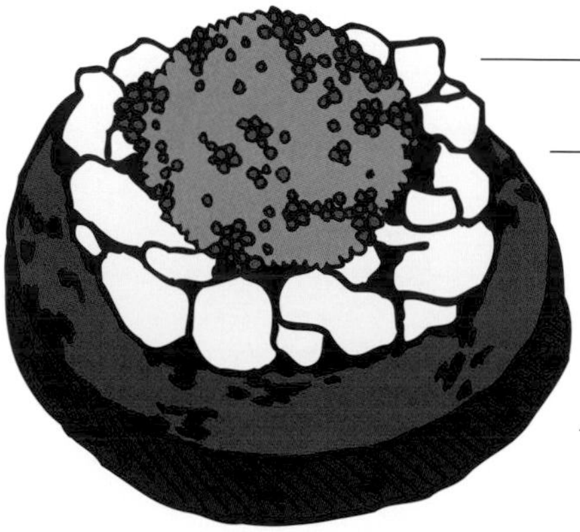

My Favorite Molds

Date: _____

Occasion: _____

_____

Guests: _____

_____

_____

_____

_____

Menu: _____

_____

_____

_____

_____

_____

_____

_____

_____

_____

_____

_____

_____

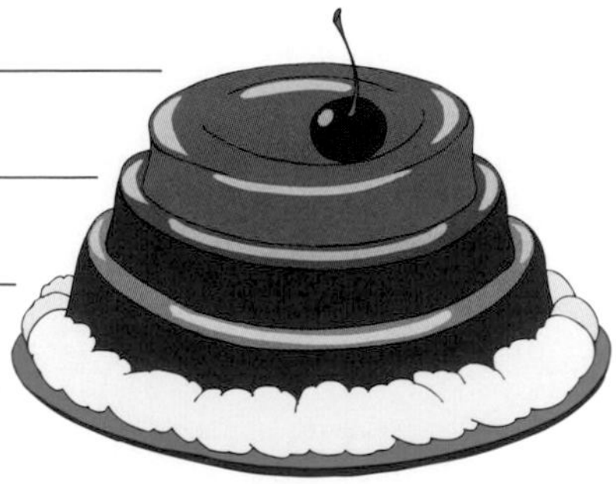

My Favorite Molds

Date: _____

Occasion: _____
_____

Guests: _____
_____
_____
_____
_____

Menu: _____
_____
_____
_____
_____
_____
_____
_____
_____
_____
_____
_____

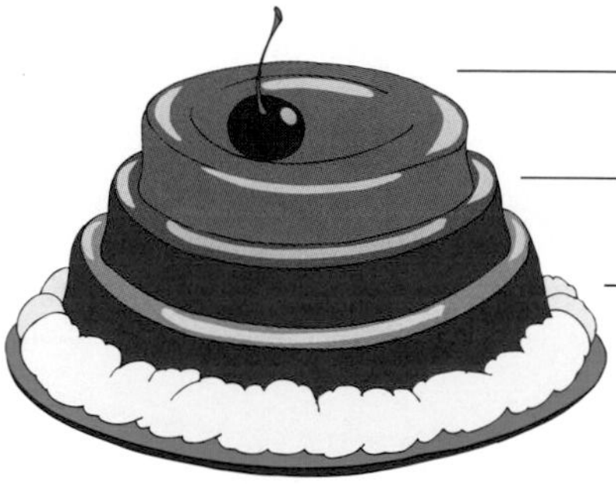

My Favorite Take-Along Treats

Date: _____

Occasion: _____

_____

Guests: _____

_____

_____

_____

Menu: _____

_____

_____

_____

_____

_____

_____

_____

_____

_____

_____

My Favorite Take-Along Treats

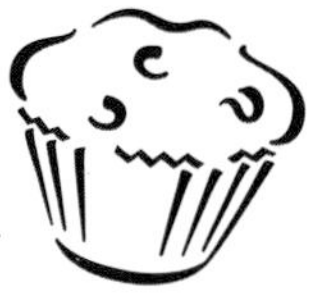

Date: ______________________________

Occasion: ______________________________

____

Guests: ______________________________

____

____

____

____

Menu: ______________________________

____

____

____

____

____

____

____

____

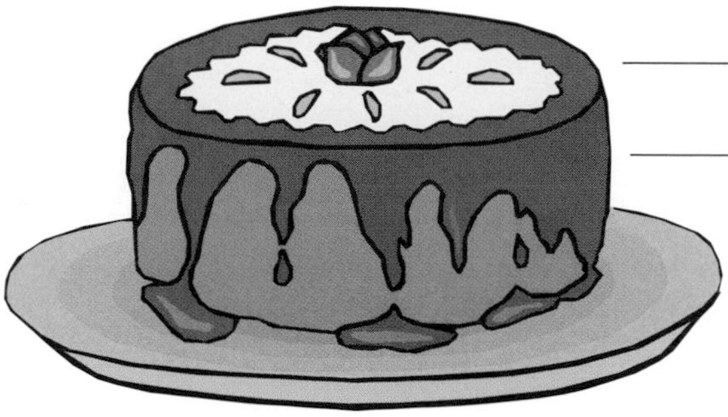

____

____

____

____

My Favorite Take-Along Treats

Date: _____

Occasion: _____
_____

Guests: _____
_____
_____
_____
_____

Menu: _____
_____
_____
_____
_____
_____
_____
_____
_____
_____
_____

My Favorite Take-Along Treats

Friend: _____

Date: _____

Food Gift: _____

_____

_____

_____

_____

_____

_____

_____

_____

_____

_____

_____

_____

_____

_____

_____

_____

269

My Favorite Take-Along Treats

Friend: _____

Date: _____

Food Gift: _____

_____

_____

_____

_____

_____

_____

_____

_____

_____

_____

_____

_____

_____

_____

_____

_____

Friend: _____

Favorite foods: _____

_____

_____

_____

_____

_____

Don't serve: _____

_____

_____

_____

_____

_____

_____

_____

_____

_____

_____

My Favorite Friends

Friend:

Favorite foods:

Don't serve:

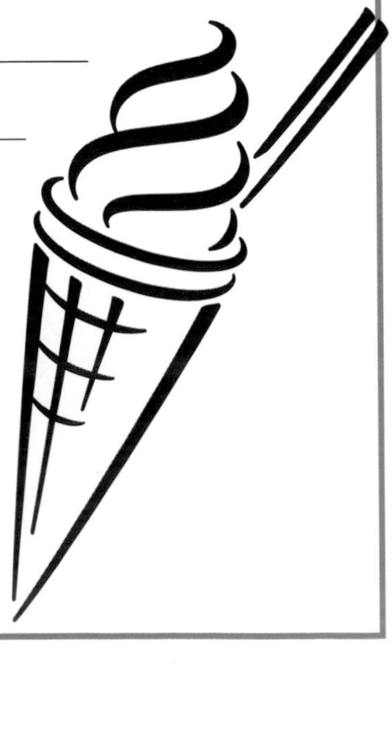

Hints, Tips & Index

Tips & Techniques

All of the recipes appearing in this publication have been developed and tested by the food professionals in the JELL-O Test Kitchens to ensure your success in making them. We also share our JELL-O secrets with you. These foolproof tips, many with step-by-step photos, help you get perfect results every time.

GELATIN

Making JELL-O Brand Gelatin Dessert is easy. Just follow the package directions and the results will be a success.

The basic directions as written below are also on the package:

- Stir 1 cup boiling water into 1 package (4-serving size) gelatin at least 2 minutes until completely dissolved. Stir in 1 cup cold water. Refrigerate 4 hours or until firm. (For an 8-serving size package, use 2 cups boiling water and 2 cups cold water.)

- JELL-O Brand Sugar Free Low Calorie Gelatin Dessert is prepared in the same way. It can be used in many recipes that call for JELL-O Brand Gelatin Dessert.

Some tips for success

- To make a mixture that is clear and uniformly set, be sure the gelatin is completely dissolved in boiling water or other boiling liquid before adding the cold water.

- To double a recipe, just double the amounts of gelatin, liquid and other ingredients used, except salt, vinegar and lemon juice. For these, use 1½ times the amount given in the recipe.

- To store prepared gelatin overnight or longer, cover it before refrigerating to prevent drying. Always store gelatin desserts and molds in the refrigerator.

- Generally, gelatin molds are best served right from the refrigerator. A gelatin mold containing fruit or vegetables can remain at room temperature up to 2 hours. Always keep a gelatin mold containing meat, mayonnaise, ice cream or other dairy products refrigerated until ready to serve. Also, do not let it sit at room temperature longer than 30 minutes. Store any leftover gelatin mold in the refrigerator.

How to Speed Up Refrigerating Time

- Choose the right container. Use a metal bowl or mold rather than glass, plastic or china. Metal chills more quickly and the gelatin will be firm in less time than in glass or plastic bowls.

- Use the speed set (ice cube) method. (Do not use this method if you are going to mold gelatin.) For a 4-serving size package, stir ¾ cup boiling water into gelatin in medium bowl at least 2 minutes until completely dissolved. Mix ½ cup cold water and ice cubes to make 1¼ cups. Add to gelatin, stirring until slightly thickened. Remove any remaining ice. Refrigerate 30 minutes for a soft set or 1 to 1½ hours until firm. (For an 8-serving size package, use 1½ cups boiling water. Mix 1 cup cold water and ice cubes to make 2½ cups.)

- Use the ice bath method. (This method will speed up the preparation of layered gelatin molds.) Prepare gelatin as directed on package. Place bowl of gelatin in a larger bowl of ice and water. Stir occasionally as mixture chills to ensure even thickening.

- Use the blender method. (This method can be used to make quick and easy layered gelatin desserts.) Place 1 package (4-serving size) gelatin and ¾ cup boiling liquid in blender container; cover. Blend on low speed 30 seconds. Mix ½ cup cold water and ice cubes to make 1¼ cups. Add to gelatin, stirring until partially melted; cover. Blend on low speed 30 seconds. Pour into dessert dishes. Refrigerate at least 30 minutes or until set. The mixture sets with a frothy layer on top and a clear layer on bottom. (Use this method for 4-serving size package only. The volume of liquid required for an 8-serving size package is too large for most blenders.)

Gelatin Refrigerating Time Chart

In all recipes, for best results, the gelatin needs to be refrigerated to the proper consistency. Use this chart as a guideline to determine the desired consistency and the approximate refrigerating time.

When a recipe says:	It means gelatin should:	Refrigerating Time:		Gelatin Uses:
		Regular set	Speed set*	
"Refrigerate until syrupy"	Be consistency of thick syrup	1 hour	3 minutes	Glaze for pies, fruit
"Refrigerate until slightly thickened"	Be consistency of unbeaten egg whites	1¼ hours	5 to 6 minutes	Adding creamy ingredients or when mixture will be beaten
"Refrigerate until thickened"	Be thick enough so that a spoon drawn through leaves a definite impression	1½ hours	7 to 8 minutes	Adding solid ingredients such as fruits or vegetables
"Refrigerate until set but not firm"	Stick to finger when touched and should mound or move to the side when bowl or mold is tilted	2 hours	30 minutes	Layering gelatin mixtures
"Refrigerate until firm"	Not stick to finger when touched and not mound or move when mold is tilted	Individual molds: at least 3 hours 2- to 6-cup mold: at least 4 hours 8- to 12-cup mold: at least 5 hours or overnight		Unmolding and serving

Speed set (ice cube) method is not recommended for molding.

Gelatin Consistencies

Gelatin should be consistency of thick syrup.

Set but not firm gelatin should stick to finger when touched and should mound or move to the side when bowl or mold is tilted.

Slightly thickened gelatin should be consistency of unbeaten egg whites.

Firm gelatin should not stick to finger when touched and should not move when mold is tilted.

Thickened gelatin should be thick enough so that a spoon drawn through it leaves a definite inpression.

The Secret to Molding Gelatin

The Mold

• Use metal molds, traditional decorative molds and other metal forms, or plastic molds. You can use square or round cake pans, fluted or plain tube pans, loaf pans, or metal mixing bowls (the nested sets give you a variety of sizes). You can also use metal fruit or juice cans. (To unmold, dip can in warm water, then puncture bottom of can and unmold.)

• To determine the volume of the mold, measure first with water. Most recipes give an indication of the size of the mold needed. For clear gelatin, you need a 2-cup mold for a 4-serving size package and a 4-cup mold for an 8-serving size package.

• If mold holds less than the size called for, pour the extra gelatin into a separate dish. Refrigerate and serve it at another time. Do not use a mold that is too large, since it would be difficult to unmold. Either increase the recipe or use a smaller mold.

• For easier unmolding, spray mold with no stick cooking spray before filling mold.

The Preparation

• To prepare gelatin for molding, use less water than the amount called for on the package. For a 4-serving size package, decrease cold water to ¾ cup. For an 8-serving size package, decrease cold water to 1½ cups. (This adjustment has already been made in the recipes in this publication.) The firmer consistency will result in a less fragile mold. It also makes unmolding much simpler.

• To arrange fruits or vegetables in the mold, refrigerate gelatin until thickened. (If gelatin is not thick enough, fruits or vegetables may sink or float.) Pour gelatin into mold to about ¼-inch depth. Reserve remaining gelatin at room temperature. Arrange fruits or vegetables in decorative pattern on gelatin. Refrigerate mold until gelatin is set but not firm. Spoon reserved gelatin over pattern in mold. Refrigerate until firm, then unmold.

The Unmolding

• First, allow gelatin to set until firm by refrigerating several hours or overnight. Also chill serving plate on which mold is to be served by storing in refrigerator.

• Make certain that gelatin is completely firm. It should not feel sticky on top and should not mound or move to the side if mold is tilted.

• Moisten tips of fingers and gently pull gelatin from around edge of mold. Or, use a small metal spatula or pointed knife dipped in warm water to loosen top edge.

• Dip mold in warm, not hot, water just to rim for about 15 seconds. Lift from water, hold upright and shake to loosen gelatin. Or, gently pull gelatin from edge of mold.

• Moisten chilled serving plate with water. (This allows gelatin to be moved after unmolding.) Place moistened serving plate on top of mold. Invert mold and plate; holding mold and plate together, shake slightly to loosen. Gently remove mold. If gelatin does not release easily, dip mold in warm water again for a few seconds. Center gelatin on serving plate.

Unmolding

1. Before unmolding, gently pull gelatin from around edge of mold with moist fingertips.

4. Place moistened serving plate on top of mold.

2. Dip mold in warm water, just to the rim, for about 15 seconds.

5. Invert mold and plate; shake to loosen gelatin.

3. Lift mold from water, hold upright and shake to loosen gelatin.

6. Remove mold and center gelatin on plate.

277

Simple Additions

Fruits and Vegetables

• Refrigerate gelatin until thickened. For a 4-serving size package, add ¾ to 1½ cups sliced or chopped fruit or vegetables. (For an 8-serving size package, add 1½ to 3 cups.) Do not use fresh or frozen pineapple, kiwi, gingerroot, papaya, figs or guava. An enzyme in these fruits will prevent the gelatin from setting. However, if cooked or canned, these fruits may be used. Drain canned or fresh fruits well before adding to the gelatin (unless a recipe specifies otherwise). The fruit juice or syrup can be used to replace part of the cold water used in preparing the gelatin.

• Some favorite fresh fruits include apples, bananas, peaches, oranges, grapefruit, melons, grapes, pears, strawberries, blueberries and raspberries. Canned fruits include peaches, pineapple, pears, apricots, mandarin oranges, cherries and fruit cocktail. Dried fruits, such as raisins, currants, figs, dates, apricots or prunes, can be added to gelatin. Nuts, such as coconut, walnuts, pecans and almonds, can also be used.

• Gelatin salads can include fresh vegetables, such as carrots, celery, peppers, onions, cucumbers, tomatoes or summer squash. Serve them on crisp salad greens.

Carbonated Beverages

Substitute cold carbonated beverages, such as seltzer, club soda, fruit-flavored seltzer, ginger ale or a lemon-lime carbonated beverage, for part or all of the cold water. (Do not use tonic water.)

Fruit Juice or Iced Tea

Use fruit juices, such as orange, apple, cranberry, canned pineapple or white grape juice, for part of the cold water. Nectars, such as apricot, peach and mango, or juice blends and drinks can also be substituted. Or, use iced tea, plain or flavored, for part of the cold water.

Citrus Fruits

Adding grated orange, lemon or lime peel and lemon or lime juice will add zing to your gelatin. Add 1 teaspoon grated peel and/or 1 tablespoon juice to a 4-serving size package of gelatin. For an 8-serving size package, use 1½ teaspoons grated peel and 1½ tablespoons juice.

Flavored Extracts

Add just a touch of flavoring extracts, such as vanilla, almond, peppermint or rum, for additional flavor.

PUDDING

The recipes in this publication use both JELL-O Cook & Serve Pudding & Pie Filling, which requires cooking, and JELL-O Instant Pudding & Pie Filling, which is not cooked. These products are not interchangeable in recipes. Be sure to use the product called for in the recipe.

JELL-O Instant Pudding & Pie Filling is also available Fat Free. Both the Instant and the Cook & Serve Pudding & Pie Fillings are also available as Sugar Free Fat Free.

See individual packages for basic directions for preparing the products as either a pudding or a pie filling.

Some Tips for Success

For JELL-O Instant Pudding & Pie Filling

- Always use cold milk. Beat pudding mix slowly, not vigorously.

- For best results, use 2% lowfat milk or whole milk. Skim, 1% lowfat, reconstituted nonfat dry milk or lactose-reduced milk can also be used. For Fat Free or Sugar Free Fat Free Pudding & Pie Filling, use cold skim milk.

- Always store prepared pudding desserts, pies and snacks in the refrigerator.

For JELL-O Cook & Serve Pudding & Pie Filling

- It's best to cook the pudding in a heavy saucepan to ensure even heating. Stir pudding mixture constantly as it cooks. Make sure it comes to full boil. The mixture will be thin, but will thicken as it cools.

- For a creamier pudding, place a piece of plastic wrap on the surface of pudding while cooling. Stir before serving.

- To cool pudding quickly, place saucepan of hot pudding in larger pan of ice water; stir frequently until mixture is cooled. Do not use this method for pie filling.

Simple Additions

- Stir mix-ins such as chopped candy bar, chopped cookies, candy-coated milk chocolate candies, peanut butter or butterscotch chips, BAKER'S Semi-Sweet Real Chocolate Chips, miniature marshmallows, nuts or toasted BAKER'S ANGEL FLAKE Coconut into prepared pudding just before serving.

- Stir fruit such as chopped banana or strawberries, raspberries, blueberries, mandarin orange segments or drained canned fruit cocktail into prepared pudding just before serving.

- For spiced pudding, stir ½ teaspoon ground cinnamon into a 4-serving size package of pudding mix before adding cold milk.

NO BAKE CHEESECAKES and DESSERTS

Some Tips for Success

- The cheesecake can also be prepared in an 8- or 9-inch square pan or 12 foil- or paper-lined muffin cups.

- Two packages of the cheesecake can be prepared in a 13×9-inch pan or a 9×3-inch springform pan.

- To serve, dip the pie plate just to the rim in hot water for 30 seconds before cutting.

- To freeze, cover the cheesecake. Freeze up to 2 weeks. Thaw in refrigerator 3 hours before serving.

- For easy cleanup, line the 8- or 9-inch square pan with foil before preparing the No Bake Dessert.

- The No Bake Desserts can also be served frozen. Freeze 4 hours or until firm. Remove from freezer and serve immediately.

I Know I Don't Have

If you don't have:	Use:
1 teaspoon baking powder	½ teaspoon baking soda plus ¼ teaspoon cream of tartar
½ cup firmly packed brown sugar	½ cup sugar mixed with 2 tablespoons molasses
1 ounce (1 square) unsweetened baking chocolate	3 tablespoons unsweetened cocoa plus 1 tablespoon shortening
3 ounces (3 squares) semisweet baking chocolate	3 ounces (½ cup) semisweet chocolate morsels
1 cup sweetened whipped cream	4½ ounces thawed frozen whipped topping
1 cup heavy cream (for baking, not whipping)	¾ cup whole milk plus ¼ cup butter
1 cup cake flour	1 cup minus 2 tablespoons all-purpose flour
1 cup honey	1¼ cups granulated sugar plus ¼ cup water
1 package active dry yeast	1 cake compressed yeast

General Substitutions

If you don't have: **Use:**

1 cup buttermilk   1 tablespoon lemon juice or
                                             vinegar plus milk to equal
                                             1 cup (stir; let stand 5 minutes)

1 tablespoon cornstarch   2 tablespoons all-purpose flour
                                             or 2 teaspoons arrowroot

1 whole egg   2 egg yolks plus 1 teaspoon
                                             cold water

1 teaspoon vinegar   2 teaspoons lemon juice

1 cup whole milk   1 cup skim milk plus
                                             2 tablespoons melted butter

1 cup sour cream   1 cup plain yogurt

Common Weights and Measures

Dash = less than ⅛ teaspoon   ¾ cup = 12 tablespoons

½ tablespoon = 1½ teaspoons   1 cup = 16 tablespoons

1 tablespoon = 3 teaspoons   ½ pint = 1 cup or 8 fluid ounces

2 tablespoons = ⅛ cup   1 pint = 2 cups or 16 fluid ounces

¼ cup = 4 tablespoons   1 quart = 4 cups or 2 pints or
                                              32 fluid ounces
⅓ cup = 5 tablespoons plus
    1 teaspoon   1 gallon = 16 cups or 4 quarts

½ cup = 8 tablespoons   1 pound = 16 ounces

How Much of This = That?

Almonds, blanched, slivered 4 ounces = 1 cup

Butter
2 cups = 1 pound or 4 sticks
1 cup = ½ pound or 2 sticks
½ cup = 1 stick or 8 tablespoons
¼ cup = ½ stick or 4 tablespoons

Chocolate
1 (6-ounce) package chocolate chips = 1 cup chips or 6 (1-ounce) squares semisweet chocolate

Cocoa, unsweetened 1 (8-ounce) can = 2 cups

Coconut, flaked 3½ ounces = 1⅓ cups

Cream cheese
1 (3-ounce) package = 6 tablespoons

1 (8-ounce) package = 1 cup

Flour
white or all-purpose 1 pound = 3½ to 4 cups
whole-wheat 1 pound = 3¾ to 4 cups

Honey, liquid 16 ounces = 1⅓ cups

Milk
Evaporated 1 (5-ounce) can = ⅔ cup
1 (12-ounce) can = 1⅔ cups
Sweetened, condensed 14-ounce can = 1¼ cups

Shortening 1 pound = 2½ cups

Sugar
Granulated 1 pound = 2½ cups
Brown, packed 1 pound = 2¼ cups
Confectioners' or powdered 1 pound = 3¾ to 4 cups, unsifted

Metric Conversion Chart

VOLUME MEASUREMENTS (dry)

$1/8$ teaspoon = 0.5 mL
$1/4$ teaspoon = 1 mL
$1/2$ teaspoon = 2 mL
$3/4$ teaspoon = 4 mL
1 teaspoon = 5 mL
1 tablespoon = 15 mL
2 tablespoons = 30 mL
$1/4$ cup = 60 mL
$1/3$ cup = 75 mL
$1/2$ cup = 125 mL
$2/3$ cup = 150 mL
$3/4$ cup = 175 mL
1 cup = 250 mL
2 cups = 1 pint = 500 mL
3 cups = 750 mL
4 cups = 1 quart = 1 L

VOLUME MEASUREMENTS (fluid)

1 fluid ounce (2 tablespoons) = 30 mL
4 fluid ounces ($1/2$ cup) = 125 mL
8 fluid ounces (1 cup) = 250 mL
12 fluid ounces ($1 1/2$ cups) = 375 mL
16 fluid ounces (2 cups) = 500 mL

WEIGHTS (mass)

$1/2$ ounce = 15 g
1 ounce = 30 g
3 ounces = 90 g
4 ounces = 120 g
8 ounces = 225 g
10 ounces = 285 g
12 ounces = 360 g
16 ounces = 1 pound = 450 g

DIMENSIONS

$1/16$ inch = 2 mm
$1/8$ inch = 3 mm
$1/4$ inch = 6 mm
$1/2$ inch = 1.5 cm
$3/4$ inch = 2 cm
1 inch = 2.5 cm

OVEN TEMPERATURES

250°F = 120°C
275°F = 140°C
300°F = 150°C
325°F = 160°C
350°F = 180°C
375°F = 190°C
400°F = 200°C
425°F = 220°C
450°F = 230°C

BAKING PAN SIZES

Utensil	Size in Inches/Quarts	Metric Volume	Size in Centimeters
Baking or Cake Pan (square or rectangular)	$8 \times 8 \times 2$	2 L	$20 \times 20 \times 5$
	$9 \times 9 \times 2$	2.5 L	$23 \times 23 \times 5$
	$12 \times 8 \times 2$	3 L	$30 \times 20 \times 5$
	$13 \times 9 \times 2$	3.5 L	$33 \times 23 \times 5$
Loaf Pan	$8 \times 4 \times 3$	1.5 L	$20 \times 10 \times 7$
	$9 \times 5 \times 3$	2 L	$23 \times 13 \times 7$
Round Layer Cake Pan	$8 \times 1 1/2$	1.2 L	20×4
	$9 \times 1 1/2$	1.5 L	23×4
Pie Plate	$8 \times 1 1/4$	750 mL	20×3
	$9 \times 1 1/4$	1 L	23×3
Baking Dish or Casserole	1 quart	1 L	—
	$1 1/2$ quart	1.5 L	—
	2 quart	2 L	—

Index

Index

Index